st Joke Book

Marty Drexler

Martin Drexler

Licensed Secondary Math
Teacher and Tutor
11 years experience

Part-time joke writer
Author, *Almost Joke Book*

Mobile/Home (330) 844-2101
drexx08@yahoo.com

VANTAGE PRESS
New York

Cover design by Susan Thomas

FIRST EDITION

Copyright © 2009 by Marty Drexler

Published by Vantage Press, Inc.
419 Park Ave. South, New York, NY 10016

Manufactured in the United States of America
ISBN: 978-0-533-15815-7

Library of Congress Catalog Card No.: 2007903563

0 9 8 7 6 5 4 3 2 1

Contents

Preface

Hello everyone, my name is Marty Drexler, a.k.a. Martin or just plain "Drex." I have many nicknames, some of which I choose not to mention at this moment. One of them is "Dictionary Boy" and I'm sure you will see why as you read through my *Almost Joke Book*. I call them "almost" jokes because they are "almost" funny. Anyway, I'm sure you can just imagine how popular I must've been in high school having such a high and mighty nickname. Yeah, I was a player. Not. At any rate, the ironic thing is that I did not acquire this nickname until just recently and it is actually one that I gave myself. Not too many people actually call me this (at least not yet anyway). I got a decent amount of my material from reading the *Oxford Dictionary* (yep, all 1008 pages), so that's why. Am I cool or what? Well, it was either that or my encyclopedia set so I figured I could get through the dictionary just a tad faster.

To give you a little background about myself, I moved a lot when I was a kid and finally settled down in a little town called Canal Fulton, Ohio by the time I reached 5th grade. My three brothers and one sister and I all went to Catholic grade school. By the time I "graduated" from 8th grade, I earned the title of "Class Clown" given to me by my peers. Of course, there were only twenty-six people in my class, so everyone had about a 4 percent chance of earning such an honor. I just have always really enjoyed making people laugh and trying to make humor out of just about anything. Speaking of my 8th grade class, I was one of only six boys so we were in a pretty cool situation. Unfortunately, I was too much of a dork to make the most of it. If those twenty girls could only see me now . . . yeah . . . uhh . . . they would see pretty much the same thing, only twenty years older. My philosophy back then was, if my material wasn't funny enough, then at least my funny looks could maybe get a smile or laugh out of them. So that brings me to one of my life mottos: If you can't be funny, then at least be funny-looking. (Just kidding of course.) As long as people were laughing, I was happy, even if it was because they were laughing *at* me.

Then came high school and you will be able to tell from some of my jokes (especially from the school-related chapter) basically what my high school experience was like. Overall it was alright I guess and by senior year, I got voted "Class Comedian" only this time my class size was 196. By now I'm starting to think that I'm actually getting pretty good at something here. Then I thought a little more and realized, yeah, getting good at being a goofball. Sweet. I came to the conclusion that being a goofball wasn't going to pay the bills (or get me a girlfriend for that matter) so I decided to go to college. I did pretty decent in my math classes so I made that my major. Yeah, it's a little hard finding comedy in mathematics so I was pretty much not funny for about five and a half years. Not even funny-looking, well, except for my pocket protector and taped up reading glasses. I graduated from Kent State University with a B.S. in Mathematics in the summer of 1997. I didn't graduate Magna Cum anything or get any special awards. There weren't any superlatives in college, but if there were I probably would've gotten voted most likely to calculate the standard deviation of some insignificant data on Friday nights. Yessireebob. I think I even did that on some Saturday nights too. What a party animal. You know, but other than that, I was pretty cool. So now here it is, 2007 and I have been teaching high school math at an inner city school for almost nine years. I've also been secretly writing some corny raps and jokes on the side that I am finally ready to share with the world. God help us all.

I finally got married at age thirty-two in the summer of '05 to my beautiful wife, Melissa, who is willing to put up with my corny jokes (at least for now). We also just had our first baby, Joshua Martin Drexler on September 17, 2006. So, all in all this is a pretty exciting time for me right now. Life is good, God is good, and I am hoping that this book will also turn out to be good. Pretty much everything in here is kid-friendly so if you're a family man or woman reading this and wondering if your child is going to pick up a dirty joke by flipping through this book then don't worry. I have fourteen nephews and nieces plus my friends have kids so the "clean" road is the one I've chosen.

Alright, I think that pretty much sums it up. Now I just invite you to kick back, relax, and enjoy some of my corny jokes and comments. If not, I hope that you at least almost enjoy them!

Acknowledgments

First off, I would like to personally thank God for all of my awesome blessings, and of course my wife, Melissa Drexler, for her extreme patience and understanding. I have invested a lot of time since these are all original "Drexisms" if you will and she has made sacrifices which I am truly grateful for. Most of these "almost" jokes have come pretty much straight out of the cornfield, that's how corny they are. I am just following the advice of one of my mentors, John "Coach" Scott (who some claim is the King of Corn), once told me: "the cornier the joke is, the funnier it is." Hey, Ohio has to be good for something and corn is definitely right up there.

I would also like to thank my family and friends who have tolerated my at times odd comments and behavior. Hopefully things will return to normal soon, at least as normal as can be expected around these here parts. Thank you all for laughing, or even pretending to laugh when my material wasn't funny enough. I appreciate you all!

Most of all, this is for my parents: Janet Drexler and (the late) Michael Drexler, Sr. You guys have done the best job in raising all five of us and we all appreciate it. Dad, we all miss you and love you very much. You guys are always in my thoughts and prayers. This book is officially dedicated to you. To my Godparents, Jim and Betty Geig, who have always been there for me through the years. Also to my grandparents on both sides: Harry and Anna Bost who have helped my mom and I tremendously over the years and (the late) Albert and Mary Drexler. Also very close to me are my siblings. Mike and his wife, Theresa, Matt, Vince and his wife Mindy, Laura and her husband Tim, and all of my beautiful nephews and nieces.

Last but certainly not least, to my six-month-old son, Joshua Martin Drexler. I'm sure I speak for everybody when I say: "Let's hope you are more like your mother than me!" OK, I think that about does it for my dedications. Now let's get on to the funny stuff already.

Almost Joke Book

One
Animals, Fish, and Insects

1. What is another word for a dinosaur?
   A thesaurus. (This one is my oldest joke.)

2. Where do kangaroos go for breakfast?
   IHOP.

3. Where do kangaroos go for dinner?
   Outback Steakhouse.

4. What is the funniest animal?
   The laughing hyena.

5. Where are laughing hyenas raised?
   On funny farms.

6. Why don't ponies ever say anything?
   Because they are always a little hoarse.

7. A black stallion ran for office one year. Critics called it a dark horse to win the election.

8. How can you tell when horses are sick?
   When they come down with hay fever.

9. A couple of horses wandered into my classroom one time and started chasing each other. I said, "Hey—hey . . . Rule #6: No horseplay." So they hung their heads and moped out of the room. I think I made them hungry when I said "hey" twice.

10. How do you know when you're bad at riding horses? If a pommel horse bucks you off.

11. Which animal is the least intelligent? The donkey: I mean, c'mon, at times this animal can be a real, well, you know.

12. What do baboons use to make shelter huts? Bamboo.

13. Bad baboons steal bamboo from other baboons.

14. Which animal is the most musically inclined? Bandicoots. (They're plant-eating marsupials.)

15. Which decade in the 20th century were lions most dominant? The roaring 20s.

16. I went to the zoo when I was a kid and I was once bitten by a shy white lion.

17. What did Billy the Goat say right before his picture was taken? Cheese.

18. Which animal is the most religious? Chipmunks.

19. Why are chipmunks so stubborn?
Because they always have a chip on their shoulder.

20. What is it called when animals constantly battle each other in the jungle?
Guerrilla warfare.

21. What happens if a cat eats too much trash?
It will have a litter.

22. Why was the Energizer Bunny arrested?
Because when he approached a red light, instead of stopping, he just kept going and going.

23. Don't mess with the Easter Bunny . . . or his peeps.

24. Bugs Bunny just proposed to his girlfriend. Sources say that the engagement ring is really nice . . . three carrots.

25. When are frogs usually born?
On leap year.

26. What was the Sugar Honey Smacks frog recently diagnosed with?
Diabetes.

27. One day a hippopotamus and a frog started a band. Do you know what kind of music they make?
Hip-hop.

28. When I was a kid, I wanted a pet puma so bad. Pumas are cool. I wanted to name it Puma. They

have such a cool name, why change it? I wanted my pet to be Puma, the puma. Pretty kitty.

29. I went on a tour of the Hoover Dam one time when I was out west. I was down at the base by the river and saw a beaver down there. I looked up at this mammoth dam, then down to the beaver, then looked back up the dam and back down to the beaver. In amazement I said, "Wow, that's some pretty impressive work there, little fellow." The beaver just looked up at me shaking his head and said, "I didn't build that, you idiot." I was like "Oh no, I know you didn't just call me an idiot."

30. Which animal is the most emotionally unstable? The squirrel. Let's face it; if you are what you eat, then these animals are just plain, well, you know.

31. When I was in college I was looking for love. I just decided, what the heck, go out on a limb. I ended up falling in love with a monkey.

32. Why are monkeys the biggest gamblers? Because they go out on a limb a lot.

33. What is the most athletic dog? The boxer.

34. True Story: Two dogs were married in London, England on September 13, 2006. Unbelievable, I know, but it happened. I've heard of puppy love but this is getting ridiculous. So who was the best man, Snoop? I heard that there was an argument between the newlyweds at the reception and the husband started

it by saying that he had a bone to pick with his wife. Other than that, everyone had a doggone good time.

35. I got a dog and I almost named him Roy. I decided to name him Ray instead. A couple weeks ago I was shopping and saw "Ol' Roy" dog food there. I almost bought it, but decided at the last minute not to. Maybe they should call it "Ol' Roy, even if your dog's name isn't Roy" dog food. If they did, then I would've bought it.

36. My biggest pet peeve is when my dog messes in the house.

37. It is too bad that "Old Yeller" had to be put to sleep. He would've been the perfect dog to sic on King Kong when the beast got loose. Double K would've been no problem for the fearless Yeller.

38. What part of Ohio has the highest population of dogs?
Licking County.

39. What is the most selfish animal?
The hog.

40. What do bears use to keep the sun out of their eyes?
Polarized sunglasses.

41. Where does an elephant keep all of its keepsakes and knick-knacks?
In its trunk.

42. What is it called when a unicorn gets shot?
A Capricorn.

43. What do female snakes use to hold up their pants?
A garter belt.

44. What did the pig say to the butcher?
"Quit bustin' my chops, cleaver boy."

45. If animals could speak, which kind would use bad words most frequently?
The fowl.

46. What is the wealthiest animal?
The ostrich.

47. Why don't baby birds ever buy anything?
Because they cheap.

48. What is another reason why baby birds never buy anything?
Because they never go shopping.

49. There was a bird that got sick one time. Do you know what it had?
The flu.

50. If the sick bird was an eagle and it broke the law, then I guess you could say it would be an ill eagle.
That was so funny I forgot to laugh.

51. What kind of bird is Catholic?
The Cardinal.

52. I just received a memo that there are snake-eating birds in Africa called "secretary birds."

53. When I was little, I had a pet owl. I named him Hu. He liked to say his own name a lot. A friend of mine came over one time, saw the owl and asked "So, who is that?"
I said "Exactly." He was a cool pet, never bothered anyone. He was pretty fly.

54. I recently bought a couple of screech owls (unlike my childhood owl). They're pretty cool but they like to screech about every half hour overnight. I live in a twenty-six-unit apartment complex. I hope my neighbors don't mind my new pets. Oh, and I forgot to tell my landlord too. I hope he doesn't find out.

55. If a buzzard ever got caught in a blizzard, it would be bedazzled.

56. Why do some birds forget to fly south for the winter? Because their minds were clouded.

57. What is the most expensive thing to buy at a pet store?
Goldfish.

58. What kind of fish is the most musically inclined?
Bass.

59. What is the most selfish fish?
Shellfish. (Try saying: "Shellfish is the most selfish fish" ten times fast.)

60. What is the most skilled and dangerous fish?
Swordfish.

61. What is the strongest fish, pound-for-pound?
Mussels.

62. What is the smartest fish?
Brain sturgeon.

63. Which fish is the handiest?
Hammerhead sharks.

64. What did the dolphin say to the whale who was crying?
"It's OK, everything will be alright. Stop blubbering."

65. A little advice: Don't ever waste your time ice fishing. I went once and I didn't get a bite . . . well, except for frostbite.

66. A very popular fish just died recently of natural causes. Many of his family members and friends went to his wake.

67. If you fillet a fish on a kitchen counter, then what kind of bacteria is most likely to be left behind?
Salmonella.

68. What does a male bee use if he wakes up with bed head?
A honeycomb.

69. Personally, I can't stand bees. If I get stung more than twice, I break out in hives.

70. What do you call a bee that pollinates a lot of flowers, but then never brags about it?
A humble bee.

71. What did the yellow jacket say to his wife the wasp?
"Honey, do you want to play a game of hive and go seek?"

72. I've been getting an overabundance of flies and bees sneaking into my apartment lately. This motivated me to go out and buy one of those flyswatters. They've been landing on food and driving me crazy with their nastiness so what I wanted to do was to train them. I'm a teacher, so naturally I want to teach them a lesson not to land on certain things. Boy let me tell you, that darn flyswatter sure does the trick. It must be working pretty well because the flies and bees don't seem to be making the same mistake twice anymore. The only drawback is that it can get a little messy sometimes. Like the other day I splattered a half-eaten ear of corn pretty good. I hope that bee enjoyed that kernel because I'm pretty sure it was his last. I'm hoping that he learned his lesson . . . what do you think?
(Now you can see why I warned you that some of these would be a little corny.)

73. What do insects do for fun in the jungle?
They play cricket.

74. What is it called when a fly flies itself into a window and dies?
It committed insecticide.

75. When most people get nervous, they get butterflies in their stomachs. Not me.
When I get nervous, I get caterpillars in my stomach. Then, about two months later the nerves go away, but then the butterflies now suddenly appear.

76. Which insect is the most religious?
The praying mantis.

77. You're supposed to identify a black widow spider by the red mark in its body. My question: "How are you supposed to analyze it to see if it's there?" I don't think these very fast and dangerous spiders are going to give you a lot of time to examine them. I don't know how you're supposed to find a red mark on a black spider anyway, even if you did have the time.

78. I was at a flea market one time and I saw someone there walking his dog. I said to him "What do you think you're doing man? You're putting your dog at risk here."
I can't believe the things people do sometimes.

79. Why are ant colonies controversial?
Because they are all nudist colonies.

80. Why is animal testing a bad idea?
Because most of them won't even be able to understand the questions since they can't read very well.

81. My neighbor's dog is a human rights activist. It rounded up all the other dogs in the neighborhood and held a peace rally at the local Humane Society. Make no bones about it . . . their voices were heard.

Two
Food

1. What is the most common choice of drink in pop culture?
   Cola.

2. Gatorade has a new drink now called "Rain." I hear it is manufactured in Seattle, WA. Firefighters like it. Sales slow down considerably during a drought and during the winter. As a matter of fact, this winter they are thinking about changing the name of the drink to, well, you know.

3. What is served every morning at the Naval Academy?
   Orange juice.

4. If naval oranges wore shirts, then what kind would they like to wear the most?
   Bare mid-riffs.

5. If you ever see a wine bottle that claims to be dry wine, then they are lying. I have bought several of these "dry" wines and have found them all to be quiet wet.

6. What is draft beer?
   Beer that gives you gas.

7. I'm hooked on Bass beer.

8. I've got some great natural spring water out by my house, however it is only available from March 21st through June 21st.

9. I wrote a really good joke a long time ago about Kool-Aid and I remember how it starts, but I forget the punch line.

10. I just met some friends of mine at a Starbucks recently. The coffee was great but man, what is up with those prices? I spent so much money there that when I talked to my wife that evening, I had to break it to her that we will not be able to take that vacation we had planned for this year . . . or next year.

11. What kind of food do chefs like the most?
    Grapes. They have a crush on them.

12. What kind of fruit do horses like the most?
    Strawberries.

13. A watermelon and a pumpkin were in love and wanted to marry, but they did not have their parents' approval. What did they do?
    They cantalouped.

14. What do you call a cucumber that is inconvenient in size, weight, or shape?
    Cucumbersome.

15. Two days after my son was born, our garden birthed some baby carrots, so we are extremely proud right now. Unfortunately, one of the carrots was born prematurely so it had to be transported to the incucumberbator.

16. I used to live just down the street from the Smucker's factory in Orrville, Ohio. The only bad thing was that I would always find myself stuck in a traffic jam.

17. I was at the hospital one time and got hungry. They brought me a PB & J sandwich, but it tasted awful. It turns out that they accidentally made me a peanut butter and petroleum jelly sandwich. The only good thing was that it helped to heal a gumboil I was suffering from at the time.

18. I made powdered doughnuts one time but I accidentally used gun powder instead of powdered sugar. About a half hour after I ate one, I got heartburn real bad. To help it, I immediately took three shots of Tequila. Pun intended.

19. A recipe for a dish that I was trying to make called for evaporated milk. I had it and I took about ten minutes prepping the other ingredients. Unfortunately by the time it came for me to put the evaporated milk in, it was gone.

20. I don't know about you, but if I hear Rachel Ray say "E.V.O.O." one more time I think I'm going to have a breakdown. Yeah, Rachael, that's nice but I'm not rich like you. I can't afford to spend $35 just to coat

my pan. I think I'll just go with regular vegetable oil. That stuff is like 95 cents a gallon.

21. A lot of people complain about being out of time or that they never have enough time. I think that is ridiculous. Whenever I am out of time, I just go to my local grocer. Thyme is usually in the spices section. I don't see what the big deal is.

22. A picture and frame fell off a restaurant wall one time. What did the head chef use to fix the cracked frame?
Tomato paste.

23. If everyone stocks up on beef stock and chicken stock then that company's stock will skyrocket in the stock market.

24. What goes good with fried summer squash?
Somersault.

25. What must your diet be very high in for you to become a professional athlete before the age of twenty?
Protein.

26. Why shouldn't you tell any secrets in a cornfield?
Because one of the ears of corn might hear you.

27. What happens if a stalk of corn gets dandruff?
It will produce cornflakes.

28. What kind of cereal do optometrists like the most?
Cornea flakes.

29. What kind of cereal will have your stomach grumbling even *after* eating it?
Quaker Oats.

30. What kind of cereal do penny pinchers like to eat?
Wheaties.

31. What cereal most closely resembles fireworks?
Rice Krispies.

32. What is the most popular cereal in China?
Rice Krispies. Maybe that explains why fireworks were invented by the Chinese?

33. What is the most popular cereal in Great Britain?
Cherrios.

34. What kind of food do divers and snorklers like the most?
It is a tie between fish sticks and submarine sandwiches.

35. What do you get if you eat too much bratwurst?
Mustard gas. Some politicians are currently testing this theory. I suppose this now raises the question: Would it be considered a chemical or a biological weapon?

36. What do you call the best looking bread roll in the kitchen?
A roll model.

37. Where would a dispute with Taco Bell be settled at?
The Supreme Court.

38. Dairy Queen had made a mistake on the name of their latest blizzard. The manager used white-out to correct it.

39. How does KFC transport its food?
    By gravy train.

40. I ate a Happy Meal while I watched *Mad T.V.* on Fox one Saturday night. I felt absolutely no emotion at all the entire time.

41. I went to Burger King one time at 11:10 A.M. and they still had their breakfast menu up. So I pull up and the lady says "Welcome to BK, would you like two sausage, egg and cheese crissandwiches for only $2.62?" I was like "Uh, no that's OK. I had breakfast like 5 1/2 hours ago. I could go for a whopper meal though but I don't know what combo number that is since all I see are egg sandwiches up here." Maybe the manager called in sick that day or something.

42. I went to Red Lobster once and it's a pretty good restaurant. The only thing was the waitress we had wasn't very nice. She snapped at me several times.

43. I went to a truck stop once off the highway that had a huge sign out front and all it said was "FOOD." So I walked in and sat down. The waitress gave me a menu and several minutes later asked me what I would like. I said, "Yeah, just go ahead and fix me a plate of food please." She said, "Well, can you be a little more specific?" I replied, "Well, I'm really hungry and you so boldly advertised that you have food here, therefore I've decided that I would really like a

plate of that." She said "OK, will that be all?" I said "No, go ahead and give me a glass of drink with it too, please." Fifteen minutes later she brought out a plate of spaghetti and I screamed "THIS ISN'T WHAT I ORDERED!" I'm just kidding. I'm a nice guy, I would never be that mean. Everything was true up until that last part. It turned out that my waitress' name was "female."

44. What do chefs use to help them cook cow tongue?
Tongs.

45. What did the baker say to the bread right before baking it?
"Waddup dough."

46. What is the best kind of food to use in a food fight?
Mussels.

47. What kind of cake hardens faster than any other kind?
Marble cake.

48. What is it called when you make a coffee cake in a muffin pan?
Coffee cupcake.

49. You *can* have your cake and eat it too, unless you're talking about a Cake CD.

50. What is Napoleon Dynamite's favorite ice cream?
Neapolitan.

51. I made corn pie one time. I called it corn cobbler. I

think that it is the only pie in the world that actually tastes better with salt and butter.

52. I ate a dreamsicle frozen treat one day. Later that night while I was sleeping, I dreamt about eating an awakesicle.

53. Why did the cookie go to the dentist?
Because it had a chipped tooth.

54. Why did the dissatisfied customer return the box of animal crackers that she just bought?
Because the seal was broken.

55. Why shouldn't kids eat too much butterscotch candy?
Because they will become drunk.

56. They actually make edible books now. I ate one last week and it took me a while to digest all of the information.

57. What two things are considered to be good brain food?
Smarties candy and Smart Choice frozen entrees.

58. Back in 2001 a candy store had a going-out-of-business sale and they had an awesome deal on miniature tootsie rolls, so I bought about 5,000. I figured I could cover Halloween for the next couple years. Well, here it is 2007 and I still have some left! I've been getting fewer and fewer trick-or-treaters lately. Sure, the tootsie rolls might

be harder than diamonds, but they still have their taste.

59. How do you know that you are at a redneck party?
When you discover that the dip for the chips is not French onion, but Copenhagen instead.

60. I was eating Sun Chips one time and I burnt my hand and mouth very severely.
I'm never eating those again.

61. What is the most popular brand of potato chip in Hawaii?
Lay's.

62. Skittles and M&Ms are the best candy—bar none.

63. There is a new dog food coming out soon that has fruity flavors and rainbow colors.
It is going to be called "Skittles-N-Bits."

Three
People

1. Do you know what Paris Hilton got on her SATs? Nail polish. Actually, her final score ended up being a 0 since she used an eye pencil instead of a #2 pencil.

2. What would Paris Hilton receive if she ever broke her arm?
A plaster of Paris cast.

3. Oh, and what is up with Paris Hilton coming out with a music CD? If she was *that good of a vocal talent, then wouldn't she have produced something* before age 25? Paris trying to magically become a singer is kind of like me trying to become a professional rugby player (I'm 6'3" about a buck seventy-five soaking wet).

4. Jessica Simpson took pictures with a disposable camera one year. When she took the last one, she went and threw the camera away. When asked why, she just said, "Well, isn't that what you do with disposable cameras, throw them away when you're done?" The interviewer asked, "Well, why even take the pictures then if you're just going to throw the camera away?" Jessica replied, "Oh, well, I don't know."

5. Pamela Anderson. There's another genius. Pam is the kind of person who will sit at the breakfast table and stare at a carton of orange juice . . . just because it says concentrate on it.

6. What kind of car does John Nash (*A Beautiful Mind*) drive?
The Infinity.

7. Simon Cowell is always looking for the "x factor." I e-mailed him once informing him that he can find it in any algebra book.

8. What was the former wrestler/current actor "The Rock" known as when he was a kid?
"The Pebble."

9. What kind of insurance does "The Rock" carry?
Prudential.

10. What does "The Rock's" diet consist of?
A high concentration of vitamins and minerals, with a heavy emphasis on the minerals.

11. A few weeks after Mel Gibson's DUI and anti-Semitic remarks, he started publicly criticizing the war in Iraq. I don't get that at all. I thought this guy was definitely pro-war. Every time I flip through the channels he is either battling 14th century England (Braveheart) or 18th century England (The Patriot).

12. What happens if Courtney Cox and David Arquette's baby gets a fever?
She will be hot CoCo.

13. When Jennifer Aniston broke up with Vince Vaughn, she asked him if they could still be friends.

14. What did Matthew Perry do after *Friends* ended?
He became an ESPN analyst and his new character's name is Scott Van Pelt.

15. What is the difference between Ben Stein and a pendulum?
Not much.

16. Ben Stein should work as a hypnotherapist. I bet he would make a pretty darn good one.

17. If Forrest Gump was a bird, what kind would he be?
A roadrunner.

18. Who should you call if your power goes out?
Carmen Electra.

19. Which actor is the fastest?
Surprisingly, it is not Jackie Chan. The correct answer is Jet Li. At times Li reaches speeds of up to 550 mph.

20. I recently found out that a stud farm is where horses are bred. Here I thought that it was where Brad Pitt and Mario Lopez were from.

21. Bob Hope brought a lot of laughter and joy to the

world with his comedy. I loved watching him perform and I had a lot of faith in his ability to make people laugh.

22. Two skeletons: Skully and Skinny were arguing over which one looked more like Nicole Richie. Skully started it off by yelling "Hey Skinny, I've got a bone to pick with you." Then I guess Skinny responded by calling Skully's a "numskull." I won't get into all the details but eventually it was resolved. Later in an interview, Skully said "Make no bones about it, I won the apartment." You might be wondering why I have skeletons in my "People" chapter and my response is:
"Hey . . . skeletons are people too!"

23. A skeleton walked up to me once and informed me that he just broke the law and was about to be arrested. I believed him too. He was dead serious.

24. What is up with female celebrities wearing those huge sunglasses that cover their whole face? I saw a picture of Nicole Richie wearing a pair and they were so big it looked like she tore the windshield off her car and strapped it to her face.

25. What did Beaver Cleaver do after the show *Leave It to Beaver* ended?
He became a butcher.

26. Martha Stewart is back on T.V. now and cooking up some new ideas on how to break the law. This time her primary objective is to see if she can actually get away with it.

27. "Dog the Bounty Hunter" has caught a lot of bone-heads who have been on the run from the law.

28. Who has the toughest job in the world? Samantha Brown. The Travel Channel pays her to travel the world and report on her sightseeing. I don't know how she sleeps at night after all the rough days that she has to deal with.

29. I got into an argument with Sponge Bob one time. He got mad when I called him "Trapezoid Pants." He thinks he won, but there were a lot of holes in his argument.

30. Sponge Bob Square Pants once used a circular saw to make a kite. He then flew it on a ship while circling the Bermuda Triangle.

31. Jamie Foxx is a pretty cool cat. He is everywhere though, doing movies, has his own T.V. show, even making hit records. You never know what he's going to do next. In short, he is a bit unpredictable.

32. Will Smith is a pretty amazing guy; I mean he can just do it all. He emerges as one of the most talented actors of his generation, all the while he is making hit CD's. Now he is a star on the New Orleans Saints defense! Man, is there anything this guy can't do?

33. The rapper/actor "Ice Cube" recently suffered a meltdown. I wasn't there or anything but apparently he was just sitting on a couch in normal room temperature and that's all it took.

34. Why haven't you heard any new music from M.C. Hammer lately?
Because he is a construction worker now.

35. I heard that M.C. Hammer is currently on a Caribbean cruise. Uhh, I hope he doesn't go overboard. If he does, he might come out M.C. Hammerhead.

36. Do you know who the first freestyle rapper was? William Wallace. Man, that dude was battling like every weekend.

37. Which female actress was the first to become a freestyle rapper?
Flo from Mel's Diner.

38. Usher is part owner of the Cleveland Cavaliers now. Does that mean that he is going to work at Quicken Loans Arena and help people find their seats? He'll be like "Hello, I am Usher and tonight I will be your, well, you know."

39. The rapper "TI" has a new song out now. It's called "Calculators." You can pick up his new CD at any music store, or even Radio Shack.

40. Sir Mix-Lot just co-wrote a song with Justin Timberlake. It is called: "Baby Got Sexy Back."

41. The rapper "Ice T" is back and he has a new partner taking the stage with him. Her name is "Lemon." I guess he figures that she'll bring a little more flavor to the show. They are going to be called "Ice T with Lemon." One of their back-up dancers is called

"Sugar." I think their next show is going to be pretty sweet.

42. What is Katt Williams' favorite song?
"I Wish" by Skee Low.

43. Who is Snoop Dogg's favorite basketball coach?
Tom Izzo (Head Coach of the Michigan State Boys Basketball Team).

44. What is Snoop Dogg's favorite type of precipitation?
Drizzle.

45. What should they change the name of Michael Jackson's "Neverland Ranch" to?
"NeverInnocent Ranch."

46. I think I want to be like Prince and turn myself into a symbol. Since I'm a math teacher, I'm thinking about going with pi (π) or infinity (∞). Lameo.

47. Who shot the sheriff?
Bob Marley. A bit of advice: Don't do what he did. It's a felony.

48. I just saw Hulk Hogan's daughter, Brooke Hogan's new video "About Us" and toward the end her girlfriends are in a verbal altercation with another group of girls. I was thinking, you know, those girls better not make Brooke mad. She might have to toss them to the ground and pull a quick double leg drop on them.

49. What is Shakira's favorite fast food restaurant?
Steak and Shake.

50. Which vacation destination did Madonna sing a song about?
Pompano Beach, Florida. ("Pampano Beach . . . I'm in so deep. Pampano Beach . . . I've been losing sleep. But I've made up my mind, I'm keeping my baby . . .") Sound familiar?

51. Which 1960's musician had the best eyesight?
Donnie Iris.

52. With all the health problems the Rolling Stones band has experienced this year, I think they should maybe change their name to the "Kidney Stones."

53. Is it just me or is Tom Petty looking more and more like Stevie Nicks nowadays?

54. First, Wayne Newton performed at the Flamingo Hilton Hotel/Casino in Las Vegas for many years. Now, Toni Braxton is the lead entertainer that took over, but she is not staying long. So now the question is, who will be the next great performer to fill the seats at the Flamingo?
I heard that it might be the "Flock of Seagulls."

55. Speaking of the "Flock of Seagulls," they really left their mark on the 80's decade. The mark that they left was basically just a nice steaming pile of bird feces. (Ok, I know, that joke stinks.)

56. How can you tell if Eddie Money is nervous?
When his voice starts sh sh shakin'.

57. Sara Beth is scared to death that she might not ever get to see Rascal Flatts perform live in concert.

58. The paparazzi has stopped taking Tom DeLonge's picture. Every time they did, his eyes were always closed. (Tom is a singer/guitar player for "Blink 182.")

59. I am proud of Taylor Hicks.

60. Is it just me or is Jeff Foxworthy and Alan Jackson the same person? Or how about Hillary Swank and Jennifer Garner? They say everyone has a twin, I guess.

61. Where was Babe Ruth from, originally?
Beirut, Lebanon.

62. Which baseball player had the most power?
Surprisingly, it was not "The Babe" . . . it was Al Kaline. (Get it?!) O.K. Maybe next year on that one. Of course, that's what they said last year and it's still not funny.

63. There was a great major league pitcher in the early 1900s by the name of Christy Matthewson. He had 373 career wins but what on earth were his parents thinking?
That is like having a daughter and naming her David.

64. What unique thing would Mickey Mantle do every Christmas?
He would hang the stockings on himself.

65. Alex Rodriguez (an infielder for the NY Yankees) had only one hit in fourteen at-bats against the Detroit Tigers in the 2006 playoffs. Yeah buddy, that's earning that $252 million Steinbrenner is paying you. In his last twelve postseason games, ARod is a mere four for forty-one for a .098 batting average! Nobody in MLB has hit that low since Chris Bando hit .086 for the 1986 Cleveland Indians. Bando was so bad that he wasn't even making the league minimum. In fact, he wasn't even on salary. Cleveland was paying him like seven bucks an hour!

66. It's got to be tough to be Todd McFarlane. He paid $3 million for Mark McGwire's 70th home run ball. At the time it seemed like a good investment since McGwire shattered Roger Maris' home run record of sixty-one that stood for almost forty years. Who knew Barry Bonds would crack seventy-three jacks three years later?! Consequently, the value of McGwire's ball dropped to $500,000. Oops. Fumble. So, the next time you think you're having a bad day, just know that someone somewhere just lost two and a half million dollars.

67. What is Jerome Bettis doing now that he is retired from professional football?
I heard that he just purchased 51 percent of Greyhound stock and is getting involved in their day-to-day operations.

68. Morten Anderson, a kicker for the Atlanta Falcons is *still* playing professional football! I thought this guy retired like fourteen years ago. I'm not saying he's old, but when he turned pro George Burns was still in high school.

69. It is true that Ryan Leaf is telemarketing now? What a bust. If having a bad attitude was against the law then he would be serving twenty-five to life.

70. I hear that Cam Cameron (former coach of the Miami Dolphins) and Kris Kristofferson (actor/country musician) are good friends.

71. Did you hear about that top college prospect named Dan Michelob? I hear that he is going to go pretty high in the draft.

72. Why does Michael Jordan like cars with standard transmissions?
Because he has always been good in the clutch.

73. What is Karl Malone doing now that he is retired from the NBA?
He is working at a Salt Lake City Post Office.

74. Is it just me, or does anyone else think that George Karl (head coach of the Denver Nuggets) and John Lithgow are actually the same person?

75. What happens to Bob Knight when he gets really tired?
He gets a little slap happy.

76. Besides being a famous inventor, Samuel Morse was also a pretty good basketball player. He had a high scoring average and always got a lot of rebounds too. The only thing was, he had a lot of his passes picked off. He had a tendency to telegraph his passes, so many of them turned into turnovers. Other than that, he was a great player.

77. Tiger Woods is *so* Good that if you're one of the best golfers in the world, you play the tournament of your life, *and* catch Tiger on an off weekend; then you might find yourself in a playoff with him. But then you will lose to him in the playoff.

78. Have you seen the new heavyweight boxing champ Nikolay Valuev from Russia?
I don't know how you could miss him. He is only seven feet tall and weighs around 325 pounds. I can't believe nobody can knock this guy out. If Muhammad Ali (who was arguably the hardest puncher in the history of boxing) was in his prime, even one of his mighty blows would merely tickle this giant. Trying to knock Nikolay out would be like starting at the bottom of Mount Everest and attempting to ski up it. His next opponent should consider eating a couple of onions right before the bout. That might be the only way he'll have a chance.

79. Carl Lewis is a good man. He has always been dependable. All his life, he has maintained a good track record. Plus, he was a pioneer in race relations.

80. Dean Karnazas ran 50 marathons in 50 days. That

is a pretty amazing feat, people. It would probably take me 50 days just to complete one marathon.

81. At the 2005 U.S. Poker Championships one of the tournament players, Lance Funston, called over a judge to seriously ask him if a flush beats three of a kind. Wow. This guy had absolutely NO business even playing in that tournament if he doesn't know that! A straight beats three of a kind and a flush beats a straight. Even I know that and I'm not even good enough to play in an amateur tournament. Lance of course won the hand and had these huge stacks of chips in front of him. Made me sick to see that. He is a perfect example of why it is better to be lucky than good to win in tournament poker.

82. There are three professional poker players that look exactly like well known actors in Hollywood. Jennifer Harmon looks just like Brittany Murphy, Phil Laak mirrors Kevin Costner, and Gus Hanson looks very much like a young Christopher Lloyd. I just thought those resemblances were somewhat amusing.

83. Once upon a time there lived a man by the name of Jack. Now, it turns out that his last name was "Clubs" and his middle name was "Of." At any rate, what do you suppose happened when he entered a Las Vegas casino?
He was carded.

84. Michelangelo painted the ceiling of the Sistine Chapel on his back. Soon after that, his girlfriend got a tattoo of the Chapel's ceiling on her back. A few

years later after they were married, and he painted his wife's tattoo on the ceiling of their home.

Someone told Vincent Van Gogh about all of this and Vince was like "What? . . ."

85. The U.S. Secretary of Education is Margaret Spellings. I guess you could say that she was just born to do *that* job. I bet that she was under added pressure to do well in her spelling bees when she was in school.

86. I know a little bit of American history. For example, Millard Fillmore from New York (the thirteenth President of the United States) was a wig. I also believe that his twin brother Harry was a toupee.

87. John Hancock was arrested and booked into jail one time. A few days later he got out on a signature bond.

88. What did Richard Nixon do after he resigned his Presidency?
He became the Mayor of Niagara Falls, N.Y.

89. Hugo Chavez, President of Venezuela and owner of Holland Oil (Citgo), has recently expressed his hatred toward America by vowing to "bring down the U.S. Government." Is he some kind of funny comedian or something? Maybe just funny-looking. Man, he can't even bring down a coffee mug from the top shelf of his kitchen cabinet. What a dork.

90. The dictator of North Korea is Kim Jong-il who is constantly in defiance of U.N. Policies. If I ever met

this clown then I would say "Hello there Kimmy, that's a pretty cute name you got there. How are you supposed to intimidate non-communist nations with such a girlish name?" I'm not afraid of this idiot. He's like 5'1" so it's no wonder that we don't see eye to eye. What's he going to do, fire a missile at me? It would probably just splash into Lake Erie or something corny like that anyway.

91. John Mark Karr turned out to be cleared of JonBenet's murder. Apparently he had imagined doing it. Police later imagined John being injected with a lethal syringe. He was driven from jail to a news conference in an unmarked car. If being an attention-getting loser was against the law, then John would definitely be serving twenty-five to life.

92. What is Heidi Klum's favorite animal?
The seal. Did you know that when it snows, seals are her power, her pleasure, her pain? Then, mysteriously, these seals deliver roses somehow. Amazing how that happens.

93. Why was Houdini never afraid to break the law?
Because even if he got sent to prison, he would just escape.

94. Joshua Cribbs is a pretty good kick return player for the Cleveland Browns. He has been playing football for a very long time, ever since he was a baby.

95. Who is the most colorful comedian?
Josh Blue.

96. Which last name has produced the biggest family tree and why?
Levi's, because they have the most genes.

97. If Mother Nature was an actual person, then what kind of bank account would she have?
A daylight savings account.

98. Who is Mother Nature married to?
Old Man Winter.

99. What did Mother Nature and Old Man Winter name their two girls?
Summer and Autumn.

100. Where is "The Sandman" from?
Las Vegas.

101. What did cavemen do on the weekends back in the day?
They hit the clubs.

102. What kind of flowers did ancient Egyptians take to funerals?
Mums.

103. What do toddlers do on the weekends?
They kick it at the crib.

104. What kind of music do toddlers like the most?
Swing music.

105. What kind of music does Santa's Elves like the most?
Rap music.

106. A boy scout once asked me if I knew the differences between hitches, bends, shanks, and bowlines. I replied "I'm afraid knot."

107. What do fishermen have in common with the fish that they catch?
They both have scales.

108. What happened to the commercial fisherman who was habitually late for work?
They docked his pay.

109. What do fishermen and T.V. broadcasters have in common?
They both work with anchors.

110. What do fishermen and football players have in common?
Tackle.

111. Why do paperboys sometimes make good wide receivers?
Because they are pretty good at running routes.

112. Why did the baseball player get arrested?
Because he stole too many bases.

113. What do baseball pitchers do if they are unhappy with their salaries?
They initiate a strike.

114. What should a baseball coach do if one of his players breaks a team rule for the first time?
He should send him to the warning track for 15 minutes to think about what he did.

115. What do professional baseball pitchers and opera singers have in common?
They both have great control of their pitch.

116. What kind of athlete bounces the most checks?
Basketball players.

117. What do basketball players get if they play too much basketball?
Whooping cough (pronounced hooping cough).

118. When basketball players are hitting all their shots, they are considered to be "in the zone" except for Larry Bird. When Bird was on fire, he was "in the ozone."

119. Which professional basketball team has the hottest cheerleaders?
The Phoenix Suns.

120. A friend of mine says that he has an M.B.A., which makes absolutely no sense to me. He's not even good at basketball.

121. What happens if you go to a lost and found and you discover a professional athlete there?
I would say that your finding would be considered to be quite profound.

122. What did the boxer have for lunch?
A knuckle sandwich.

123. What do professional boxers use when they eat cereal?
A punch bowl.

124. Why should more athletic women consider a career in professional boxing?
Because the purses keep getting bigger each year.

125. What kind of shirts do horse jockeys wear?
Polo shirts.

126. Why was the tennis club shut down?
Because the owner was arrested for racketeering.

127. Why did the gymnast become a bank teller?
Because she already had a lot of experience with vaults.

128. What did the gymnast tell her coach after making a crucial mistake at a competition?
"Sorry coach, my vault!"

129. I know a dermatologist who used to be a gymnast.
Her best event was the pH balance beam.

130. Why do exercise instructors play music during their shows?
Because that way viewers won't be able to hear them when they pass gas.

131. When you form a group of friends, why is it a good

idea to make sure that one of them is a soccer player?
Because when you all go out, soccer players are usually willing to foot the bill.

132. I took my nephews and nieces bowling one time and they had a ball.

133. After a sport event, two cameramen decided to race each other in the parking lot.
It was actually pretty close . . . they ended in a photo finish.

134. What happens if a gladiator match ends in a tie?
They go to sudden death overtime.

135. What do mountain climbers usually suffer from when they wake up on a mountain?
A hangover.

136. A mountain climber was talking to his wife on his cell phone while climbing a mountain one day. Suddenly, he told her that he would have to hang up soon. She asked him if it was because his signal was low, but he said "No, pretty soon I will be out of peak minutes."

137. How a golf caddy gets tipped varies directly to how well his golfer does on the 18th hole. The caddy could do the most perfect job for the entire round, but then on the last hole (at no fault of the caddies), this happens: The golfer hits his tee shot OB (out of bounds), then his third shot splashes in the water, and finally he four-putts the green. By now the golfer is so teed

off (no pun intended) that he smashes two clubs against a tree, breaking them and forgets completely about paying his caddy. Since tips from the golfer are pretty much the only money a caddy makes, he or she relies heavily upon them. I know this because this story is exactly what happened to me one beautiful Saturday afternoon in Ohio. Needless to say, I took an extended break after that round . . . really extended. In fact, I believe I'm still on it! That was the last day I ever worked four hours for free. The moral: Before becoming a caddy at a country club, make sure that there is no water on the eighteenth hole.

138. What sport is a farmer most likely to be knowledgeable about?
Fencing.

139. Why are farmers cool?
Because they produce produce.

140. What does an aspiring farmer need to get started?
Seed money.

141. How are farmers paid?
They are on celery pay, not hourly.

142. Farmers are important stakeholders concerning the influence of cattle prices. (Or should I spell it steakholders?)

143. What did the farmer say to his wife who kept nagging him?
"Cut me some flax, Jackie!"

144. What did his hard-of-hearing wife say back?
"Did you say that you wanted some flapjacks please?"

145. What did the farmer say to his top milk-producing cow?
"Well done."

146. What do farmers and rappers have in common?
They both make beets (beats).

147. Rappers are gifted.

148. Gifted people present themselves well.

149. I guess this means by the Transitive Property that rappers present themselves well.
Clearly this syllogism is false. Sometimes they do, but other times they just look wack. (I will cover syllogisms in more detail next chapter.)

150. There is a new rock group that is forming and all of the musicians are from Akron, Ohio. Have you heard what they are calling themselves?
"The Rubber Band." (A little northeast Ohio humor there.)

151. I knew a mime once and we met a group of mutual friends at a karaoke bar. I talked him into going up there and performing "Little Wing" by Stevie Ray Vaughn. He actually did quite well. (For those of you who are unfamiliar with SRV, "Little Wing" is an instrumental.)

152. Why did the one-man-band all of a sudden decide to become an airline pilot?
Because he felt that he could handle all of the instruments.

153. What does a pilot do if his flaps aren't working properly?
That means that he will just have to wing it.

154. Where do pilots and astronauts bank at?
Sky bank.

155. Why did the comedian go to the crafts store?
Because he was looking for some funny material.

156. What do chefs, stock boys, and newspaper truck drivers have in common?
They all work with their pallets a lot.

157. What is the new line of clothing for chefs called?
Cookware.

158. My friend Sue went to culinary school several years ago. She is now working as a Sous Chef at a local restaurant. I guess she was born to be in that line of work. Unfortunately she recent made a mistake on somebody's dinner and I heard that they threatened to sue.

159. Of all the professions out there, why are bakers the poorest?
Because they always knead dough.

160. What do bakers and policemen have in common when they first arrive at work?
In both jobs, roll call is taken right away.

161. In Columbus, Ohio there is a police officer that is 6'10" (don't ask me how I know that). I guess this gives a whole new meaning to the term "Long arm of the law."

162. If an unlawful person hires a clown for a party, how does he pay him?
With funny money.

163. A prisoner who was in jail for credit card fraud recently passed away (from natural causes). Authorities said that he will be buried in debt.

164. I was arrested by the secret police one time. Shh, don't tell anybody.

165. Why do police officers sometimes need the help of hair stylists?
Because when they need to comb the streets to find a fugitive, hair stylists sometimes come in handy.

166. What do police do if they discover that someone has stolen a bee farm?
They set up a sting to provoke the arrest.

167. I don't understand how there can be so many shoplifters out there. I tried to be one once and I just couldn't do it. Have you ever tried lifting an entire shop off its foundation? Trust me, it's pretty tough.

168. There was a drug bust at a local bowling alley recently. Several local dealers were arrested, including one who is thought to be the kingpin.

169. True story that I saw on the news: Someone was arrested for having too many overdue books at the library. The library's official policy is: If you don't return your books on time, fine. Man, they weren't kidding. Hey, don't mess with those deceptive library ladies. They'll have the law throw the book at you. Next thing you know, you're getting booked into jail. OK, I'm done with the book thing now.

170. Why would librarians make good poker players?
Because they would probably read their opponents well.

171. Why would plumbers make good poker players?
Because they know how to make a flush. Or, if they get crappy cards, they know what to do with them.

172. What is it called when a beginning plumber with no formal training begins servicing customers?
He is in a sink or swim situation.

173. I got into a pretty heated debate with my furnace man one time. He thought that I needed a new furnace and I argued that I just needed my ducts cleaned. After a while I just told him to chill out.

174. Why are trash collectors cool?
Because they rarely refuse refuse.

175. What do models and trash collectors have in common?
They both work a lot with waist (waste). Actually, I think I should trash that joke.
What do you think?

176. What does a miner need to do to be successful?
He or she would make sure to set good short and long term coals, then go out and achieve them. Wow. That might just be the corniest joke ever right there. I'm surprised that one made the cut.

177. Why don't coal miners ever run for office?
Because their opponents would have no problem digging up a lot of dirt on them.

178. I dig archaeologists.

179. What did the archaeologist say to his family right when they all sat down for dinner?
"OK, gang, dig in."

180. What happens if a construction worker doesn't pay his rent?
He gets excavated.

181. What is the end result if a construction worker tells a funny joke?
An orange barrel of laughs.

182. Which country has the most construction workers?
Ukraine.

183. Which nationality is always in the biggest hurry?
The Russians.

184. I think that meteorologists are pretty cool . . . especially in the winter.

185. What game is usually played when a meteorologist throws a party?
Twister.

186. My neighbor has State Farm insurance.

187. What do Arabs use to write letters to their pen pals?
Sandpaper.

188. I tell you, it feels great to finally have a best friend. I've had friends in my life, but never a best friend. I was listening to the radio the other day and I was informed by a commercial that George Waikem is my best friend. It goes "George Waikem Ford is your best friend . . . " That's so cool . . . George, buddy, glad to have you for my best friend (even though I've never even met you). Hey, you're the owner of a big car dealership. You must have some extra cash. Can you let me hold about ten grand for a minute? You know, since we're best friends and everything. I'll send you ten dollars a month to pay you back.
What do you say, buddy?

189. A long time ago when my girlfriend broke up with me, she was giving me the whole "It's not you, it's me . . ." speech. All I could say was "Well duh. What would a female sheep have anything to do with our

problems anyway?" (Get it . . . you sounds like ewe.) The argument just escalated at that point.

190. Which two restaurants are the Royal Family's favorite?
Burger King and Dairy Queen.

191. I knew a girl in college and her name was Sharon. She was very selfish though.
Hey, isn't that an oxymoron?

192. Why should computer programmers also make good dancers?
Because they have a lot of algorithm.

193. I have a group of aunts who play cribbage religiously. I mean, they play so much that I think they just go way overboard with it. Take the other night for example.
They all took a break from the game, went into the kitchen and made stuffed cribbage from scratch. Ridiculous man.

194. Why would Eskimos make good painters?
Because they would know exactly how many coats you need.

195. What do composite artists do?
They make paintings of numbers that are not prime.

196. There is an interior designer that I met once. She came across as a very strict person. (How strict was she?)
She was so strict that she made people present their I.D. at her border.

197. There's a business plaza near where I live that has a motivational speaker's office right next to a mortician. They bumped into each other in the parking lot one day and I witnessed their conversation. The motivator said to the mortician "Hey there, neighbor! So, how many deaths this week?" The mortician said "Six." The motivator then cheerfully replied "Well, let's hope for a dozen next week!" The mortician mumbled back "Whatever, sicko."

198. Which card game was originally invented by a bartender?
Gin Rummy.

199. What did the ballerina get for Christmas?
Mistletoe shoes.

200. One year I brought a Christmas present for my mom at "Things Remembered." I forget what I got her though.

201. What would you call a person who is lost and sad, wandering aimlessly on the streets of South Korea?
I would say that this person is doing some Seoul searching.

202. Why did the tourist get lost trying to find historic Gettysburg?
Because he had lost the address.

203. What happens if a conductor (or engineer) is telling you a story about the railroad and suddenly forgets the ending, leaving you hanging?
His train of thought must've derailed.

204. Why did the conductor wreck his locomotive?
Because he was not *trained* properly.

205. What did the priest say to the puzzle right before he started working it?
Piece be with you.

206. I'm a big fan of the "Miss America Plus Size" pageant.

207. What do we know about a guy named Lou who rents an apartment?
To his landlord, he is a Lieutenant.

208. My masseuse is a part-time comedian. I think that she is starting to rub off on me.

209. A recent statistic shows that 76 percent of all Americans don't like change. Huh, that's weird. I do. I welcome it. I keep all of mine in a tin container. Yeah, I just rolled up like $100 worth the other day. So, if you're reading this and you're part of that 76 percent then I'll take your change.

210. What did the roller skater say to the other roller

skater who was skating toward her at a perpendicular angle?

"Why are you coming at me sideways, fool?"

211. What's up with the term "French Canadian?" Well, duh. Or should I say
"Well, eh." Isn't that like saying "Wet water?"

212. "What's up with all these high school kids driving BMW's and everything? No wonder some teens today are *so* lazy. Why work if everything is handed to you? You can always tell where the teachers park at the high school. Their lot is the one with all of the Chevy Caveliers and Geo Metros.

213. Some teenagers these days are so hard-headed, especially in the city. Trying to get some of these kids to change their attitudes is like trying to teach a mime how to be a ventriloquist.

214. What is the difference between an optimist and a pessimist?
An optimist would say, "Today is the first day of the rest of your life." A pessimist would say, "If you die tonight, then today will go down in history as being the last day of your life."

215. How do you know if someone is a pessimist?
If when given the opportunity to look at new pictures, he or she chooses to look at the negatives instead.

216. What do secretaries usually say to guys when turning them down?
"Sorry, but you're just not my type."

217. Single ladies. Beware of men with the last name "Samsonite." I hear they come with a lot of baggage.

218. What disease affects many more men than women?
Foot and mouth disease.

219. Where did the optometrist take his wife for New Year's Eve?
The Eye Ball.

220. What do eye doctors have in common with teachers?
They both work with pupils.

221. I just think that it is an incredible feat if someone goes to college for eight years and becomes a podiatrist.

222. My family doctor is hilarious. He always has a joke when I see him. One time he really had me in stitches.

223. A dentist and a carpenter were working together on a project one time but they weren't getting along at all. They were putting in some new cubicles in the dentist's office but their personalities clashed the whole time. After a couple of hours they were really going at each other tooth and nail.

Four
School-Related

1. Teachers subject students to many different subjects in school, all of which are subject to their counselor's approval.

2. What did the chalkboard say to the chalk ledge?
"I'm bored."

3. What did the chalk ledge say back?
"I'm not bored. I'm living on the edge."

4. What did the teacher do when he witnessed this conversation?
He started talking to himself like a crazy person. Then a few days later, checked himself into a mental institution. (Gee, that wasn't me, was it?)

5. What should you do if you run out of line paper?
Use lemon paper.

6. Someone asked to borrow some scratch paper once. I said "OK, but be careful, it itches."

7. Which music group is the most educated?
98 Degrees.

8. They're building a new allotment near where I live and the main road leading in is called "Education Street." I took a drive down it the other day and I learned a lot.
I've heard of street smarts but this is getting ridiculous.

9. At a local school there was a staph infection breakout. No students were affected, but several teachers reported having the virus.

10. What did the basketball say to the gym teacher? "You might as well mark me absent right now 'cause I'm about to bounce."

11. There was a high school basketball team one time that had a pirate on the team. He wasn't the mascot either! This was an actual player. In fact he was a pretty good one too. Do you know what his best shot was?
The hook shot.

12. I understand that there was a skeleton on the same team. He was deadly with the elbow shot.

13. A year later, a clown tried out for the team and made it. He took a lot of circus shots but only made a few.

14. I wasn't very bright when I was young. When the teacher said that we could write in cursive, I thought that meant we were allowed to write bad words. Actually, being the perfect child that I was, I never even tried such things.

15. My hearing wasn't very good when I was a kid. My art teacher announced once that we were going to make something out of papier-mâché the next day. I thought she said pirate machete and since I had one, I decided to bring it in as a model. Turns out that it's not a good idea to bring lethal weapons to school. Consequently, I got suspended for ten days. This was before "zero tolerance." These days they will toss you in JDC for something like that. The moral: If you're not sure what your teacher said, then raise your hand and ask them to repeat it.

16. Speaking of art, my grade school art teachers would always get so aggravated with me. The only thing I would ever draw was a house. My art teacher would always write on my paper "Would you PLEASE draw something different next time." So the next time came and I would draw a different house. She thought I was doing it on purpose just to be sarcastic but honestly at the time that was about the only thing I could draw (well enough that someone else would be able to recognize what it was). My art teacher also thought maybe I would become an architect when I grew up, so she tried to get me to draw a room. Uhh . . . no. Rooms, no can do. Just the outside of a house. At the end of the year she awarded me with "Most Predictable Artist." My parents were so proud, only because I told them that I won an art award.

17. When I was in fourth grade, my teacher was showing us examples of synonyms. She called on me to come up with one. I said, "OK, well, just this morning I had synonym toast with my eggs for breakfast.

Does that count?" I think she thought twice about calling on me after that.

18. I was a little sarcastic sometimes when I was a student. My fifth grade teacher was drilling the class and she called on me asking me what 8 × 7 was. I said "Well, you're the teacher, shouldn't you know? What are you asking me for? I should be the one who's asking you." Then she said that she just wanted to know if I knew my times tables (after she scolded me of course). So then I said "No, but I know my times chairs pretty well."

19. When I was in sixth grade I wrote my first research paper and it was on butterflies. There were several books that I skimmed through including one on the "swallow-tail" butterfly. Needless to say, it took me quite a while to digest all of the information on it.

20. When I was in seventh grade, I had to do a report on the history of minnows. So what I did was I went to the library and researched minnows on the microfiche. (Just when you don't think I could possibly get any cornier. If that one doesn't make you put the book down, I don't know what will!)

21. When I was competing in my eighth grade spelling bee, I misspelled the word misspell. What a messed up way to go out. Later that night, the conversation with my parents (who couldn't go since it was held during the school day and they were working) was like a clip from "Who's On First." My mom asked me if I won and I told her that I didn't. Then she asked "So, what word did you misspell?" So I said, "Gee

mom, funny you should ask." She said "Well, what word was it?" I replied "Misspell." Then she came back with "Yeah, that's what I asked, what word did you misspell?" This went back and forth for a good 5–10 minutes until we both finally gave up.

22. My ninth grade algebra teacher asked me to find "y." I told him my answer was "Because."

23. When I was in high school I learned how to read music. I've read several music books containing hundreds of songs and I have to tell you, I have personally found music to be slightly more entertaining to listen to than to read.

24. In my high school biology class I learned that there are thirteen parts that compose the human brain. I just can't remember what they are.

25. When I was sixteen I was taking trigonometry and studying for the written potion of my drivers test at the same time. Needless to say, I got my signs confused. As luck would have it, I ended up taking both tests on the same day. On my trig test I was writing about yielding and on the drivers test I wrote opposite over hypotenuse. Only I cold pull off such a bonehead move with such precision at that time.

26. I was definitely not the brightest bulb in the room when I went to school. An example: When my English teacher asked me what a syllogism was, I thought she was asking me how many syllables does the word symbolism have. So my answer to her question was four. Even if she was asking that, the

correct answer would've been three. What I should've said was "All the actors are cool. Paul Reubens (Pee Wee Herman) is an actor. Therefore Paul Reubens is cool." (This syllogism is clearly false.)

27. One time when I was in high school, I got jumped by a gang. Literally. They didn't come at me with baseball bats though. They used, get this . . . jumper cables to slap me around with. It must've worked too because I was really charged up and mad. I yelled "Whoa—Hey—Don't even get me started." (Ha . . . get it? Cables . . get me started! Corny.)

28. Back in high school I was 6'3" about a buck fifty-five, so you could say that I made a pretty horrible football player. By the time I was a senior, I finally made the J.V. team. That year, I proceeded to lead the league in fumbles and most bench minutes. Oh, and I was among the league leaders in concussions suffered too. The only time I made the crowd cheer was when we were playing an *away* game.

29. Cincinnati Moeller High School always has a great football team every year. They win because they hold their opponents to very few points. In short, their defense has a lot of teeth to it.

30. My high school basketball coach was pretty strict. He told us that if we missed a free throw during a critical game, then he would take us out behind the school to the guillotine. He was a real pain the neck.

31. There is a high school that I was reading about one

time whose mascot is the ghost. That's right, the Galloway Ghosts. I understand that the students there have a lot of school spirit. Attendance is a problem there though. Many kids claim that they were at school but have been mysteriously marked absent.

32. Yep, the good old high school glory days. I was such a math nerd back then that they called me the "human calculator." That alone got me a ton of dates. Not. Actually, I needed a real calculator to total up the number of times I got shot down in four years.

33. When I was a senior in high school I knew that I was going to college, but I didn't know what my major would be. I read the descriptions of every major in the catalog and one of them caught my eye. (No, it wasn't optometry.) I thought about majoring in cryptography, but I couldn't really understand the description in the catalog. I later found out that it was written in code.

34. Finally I made it to college and while I was there I read a book on microgravity. It started out slow, but by chapter three it really started to pull me in. Then I read a book called *Zero Gravity* after that. Man, I tell you, I just couldn't put that one down!

35. *Gone With the Wind* was a pretty good book. I read it while I was in line to register for fall semester my freshman year in college. Yeah, I love waiting in long lines. So, 6 1/2 hours later I'm almost finished with the book when I finally hear those beautiful words "Next please." I showed the registrar which

classes I wanted and she says to me "I'm sorry, but you have to Pre-register by phone first." I was like "Whoa, hold up, you mean I've got to register before I register?" Ridiculous man. The only good thing was I got to read a good book and I liked it so much that I bought another copy so I could read it again.

36. When I took a topology class in college, we didn't really solve any problems. We just examined the circumstances surrounding them. I guess you could say that we never really got to the bottom of it.

37. While studying to be a teacher, one of my professors told our class over and over to "expect the unexpected." So now, as a teacher, every day I prepare myself and my class for a spaceship to land on top of the school. Forget the fire drill, we practice the alien drill. When my students ask what this is all about, I tell them that my college professor convinced me that THE ALIENS ARE COMING!! That's not taking what he said out of context or anything is it? Maybe he should have been more specific considering that there were people like me in his class.

38. In college, I took a class called "Seven Ideas That Shook The Universe." Most of our focus was on the Milky Way although I can't recall ever locating any chocolate or caramel. The next semester we studied our neighboring galaxy, Snickers.

39. I wrote a book on how to publish a book, but I can't seem to get it published. I guess that goes to show you how good it must be.

40. If school books could talk, then which ones would be the loudest and why?
Math books. Because they have the most decimals.

41. I have a lot of good books and I was taking an inventory recently. However, I can't seem to find my copy of *Ghost* by King Leopold.

42. I read *The Wall Street Journal* mostly for the breathtaking pictures.

43. What is the most popular subject studied in the Middle East?
Al-Gebra.

44. Why is it a bad idea to argue with a sphere?
Because you'll just keep going around and around.

45. I have a simple two-step problem solving process that I claim will solve <u>any</u> math problem. Here it is:
Step 1) Avoid repeating yourself. Do not say the same thing over and over again.
Step 2) See Step 1.
Yep, that's it. So what do you think? I invite you to give this technique to your favorite blonde sometime and let me know how it works out for her.

46. I have found that most students don't have much interest in calculating compound interest. Maybe it should be called compound lack of interest.

47. Why are most statistics teachers mean?
Because they constantly have to calculate it. If you had to figure out averages all the time, then you

might not be very nice either. (I don't teach statistics, but I know a few people who do.)

48. What is it called when a religious algebra teacher tells a story?
It is called a parabola.

49. What is the only line that is not straight?
The coastline.

50. What do you call a math book about functions that is no longer published?
It is discontinuous.

51. What is the smartest object in geometry and why?
A ninety degree angle, because it is always right.

52. Where do squares originate from?
Square roots.

53. You can always count on Math teachers.

54. Why is it not a good idea for an English teacher to date a Social Studies teacher?
Because they just wouldn't have any Chemistry.

55. Why can you also count on English teachers?
Because they are very punctual.

56. One word is two words.

57. How do u and i communicate?
They send letters to each other.

58. Y do u and i send letters to each other?
Because they risked getting viruses with e-mail.

[Disclaimer: For numbers 59–89, these are obviously not the official Oxford Dictionary definitions. I was just inspired to write jokes on some of these words after seeing them in there.]

59. What is the definition of a bounty hunter?
It is someone who tracks down and captures paper towels.

60. What is the definition of a ceiling fan?
It is someone who loves their ceiling more than any other part of their house.

61. What is the definition of coincide?
In linear algebra, it is what happens when two lines are out in the cold without their coats. They choose to "coincide" where it is warmer.

62. What is the definition of coplanar?
It is when two or more people fly on the same airplane.

63. What is the definition of happy camper?
The former Arizona Cardinals football coach, Dennis Green, on October 17, 2006.
This is the day after blowing a 20–0 lead against the mighty 5–0 Chicago Bears on Monday Night Football. The final score was: Chicago 24 Arizona 23.
Oops.
Fumble.

64. What is the definition of marine biology?
It is the study of animals that are trained in paw-to-paw combat.

65. What is the definition of a morning dove?
It is a dove that has suffered many personal losses in his or her lifetime.

66. What is the definition of notion?
It is what happened when you're all out of lotion.

67. What is the definition of an oxymoron?
It is a teenager who breaks out a lot but is too stubborn to use oxy pads.

68. What is the definition of a paradigm shift?
It is what happens when you take two dimes and roll them on a hard surface.

69. What is the definition of paradox?
It is something that a boat pulls in-between after a long day out on the water.

70. What is the definition of pathology?
It is the study of mazes.

71. What is the definition of a pawn shop?
It is a store that is very popular in urban settlements where the buying and selling of chess game pieces takes place on a regular basis.

72. What is the definition of photosynthesis?
It is the process by which pictures are developed, usually occurring in a dark room.

73. What is the definition of a projectile?
It is someone who is a professional jectile.

74. That obviously begs the question: Who in the world is a profession jectile?
I have no idea but whoever they are, they must be pretty good at what they do.

75. What is the definition of a rectangular prism?
It is a place where bad rectangles go that broke the law. (That joke is so bad that maybe it should be sent to rectangular prism.)

76. What is the definition of a security leak?
It is what happens when the Director of Homeland Security urinates.

77. What is the definition of seismology?
It is the study of clothes.

78. What is the definition of sick pay?
It is a paycheck that is much smaller than you expected from massive taxes and pension deductions that it just makes you nauseous.

79. What is the definition of sohcahtoa?
It is a word that originates from the Native American language and actually translates into "trigonometry."

80. What is the definition of a step ladder.
It is a ladder whose biological mother marries something other than its biological father.

81. What is the definition of a surtax?
It is a tax that is only charged to men.

82. What is the definition of sushi?
It is a lawsuit that is only brought against women.

83. What is the definition of tangent?
It is a guy who stays out on the beach or at the pool during the summer for an extended period of time.

84. What is the definition of a tax-sheltered annuity?
It is a house that is owned and occupied every year by a CPA.

85. What is the definition of teepee?
Most people think that it is some kind of tent but it is actually what someone does after they drink too much tea.

86. What is the definition of trespass?
It is what happens when a quarterback completes three consecutive passes.

87. What is the definition of turnpike?
It is a fish that does not swim straight.

88. What is the definition of xenophobia?
It is the fear of Xena, the princess Warrior.

89. According to the *Oxford Dictionary,* the definition of hessian is: "A strong coarse sacking made of hemp or jute." OK, what? You know it is a pretty confusing word when the definition is only nine words and you have no idea what two of them mean.

90. According to the *Oxford Dictionary,* the definition of past master is: "A person who is especially adept or expert in an activity, subject, etc." This whole time I thought that a past master was simply some kind of historian. So many interesting facts you can pick up simply by leafing through a dictionary. I am such a winner.

91. According to the *Oxford Dictionary,* the definition of phonograph is: "An instrument that reproduces sound by a stylus that is in contact with a rotating grooved disk." I'm sure you were just dying to know that. Anyway, until I read that, I thought that a phonograph was just a picture of a telephone.

92. According to the *Oxford Dictionary,* the definition of sublime is: "Of the most exalted or noble kind, awe inspiring." Huh, here all along I thought that it was some green fruit aboard a submarine.

93. According to the *Oxford Dictionary,* the definition of vitreous humor is: "A transparent jellylike tissue filling the eyeball." On a personal note, I really don't see what is so funny about that.

94. Prefixation has a prefix of "pre" and a suffix of "tion." Personally, I prefer prefixes.

95. Why can't male pronouns ever stay in a relationship for very long?
Because many of them can be quite possessive.

96. What is the difference between macroeconomics and microeconomics?
One vowel.

97. Science teachers are really in their element when they're conducting a lab-based lesson in their area of expertise.

98. If a scientist is performing nuclear fission, then what should be used for bait?
The electric worm.

99. Carbon dioxide vs. carbon monoxide. It's amazing how one single atom of oxygen can mean the difference between life and death.

100. Nitrogen is so dominant in the atmosphere that it is even abundantly present during the day.

101. Which scientific element is the least intelligent?
Boron.

102. Which scientific element is the most protective?
Copper.

103. Two chemists were working in a lab. One said to the other "So, what do you want to work with today . . . solids, liquids, or gases?" The other chemist replied "Oh, it doesn't matter."

104. How did Judge Judy do on her science fair project back when she was in grade school?
She took Honorable Mention.

105. I wanted to know what I got in my 7th grade science class one day so I dug my old report card out of my scrapbook. Unfortunately the grade was so old that it had fully decomposed. I could read all of my other grades fine, just not my science grade.

106. What is the smartest heavenly body and why? The sun. Because it has the most degrees.

107. When will the global warming problem be solved? In about two billion years when the sun burns out.

108. What will take the place of the sun in the solar system when it burns out? The grandson will.

109. The stable balance between water pressure and air pressure is called buoyancy. An unstable imbalance is called post relationship girlancy.

110. What does Colorado have in common with carbon monoxide? They are both abbreviated CO. A geographer sees one thing, and a chemist sees another.

111. Why is Columbus the capital of Ohio? Because the headquarters for Nationwide Insurance Company is located there, and they have a lot of capital. Just ask them.

112. I heard a country music song on the radio the other day that said something about someone having some beachfront property in Arizona. I thought "Well, I'm no geography genius or anything, but I'm

pretty sure that the only sand in Arizona is pretty much desert sand, not beach sand."

113. If you ever take a photography class, what should you use to help you get an A?
Flash cards.

114. I've been working at a pretty rough inner city high school for the last eight plus years and it is a crazy scene pretty much every day. Fights are breaking out everywhere, we have three police officers on duty every day, and that's just the staff meetings. Yep, we have a pretty divided faculty, especially the math department.

115. It was really hot in my classroom one day (since my school doesn't have air conditioning) and one of my students said "Dang Mr. Drex, it's bakin' up here today." I replied "Well, I guess that only makes sense since it was sausage up in here yesterday . . . and I'm thinking that it might be ham tomorrow."

116. One of the principals at my school is Mr. Proctor. He is always in charge of administering and supervising all of the standardized tests.

117. My students freestyle rap a lot. I tell them that when I was in high school, I used to freestyle too. I did the 400 meter freestyle on my swim team. They just look at me real weird and roll their eyes when I say stuff like that. It feels so good to finally be starting to fit in.

118. My students used the word "based" a lot. Like if

something is messed up, "that's based." I tell them "My speakers are based." Or I will say "Don't based her, she's not a turkey."

119. One year I had a student named Ashleigh Watts. She was one of the brightest students in the school.

120. Another year I had one named Tramaine Fleetwood. I called him: Tramaine Cadillac Fleetwood Mac Daddy.

121. That same year, I had a female student named Constance Linear. Needless to say, she did quite well in her Algebra I class.

122. The following year, I had a girl named Daytoya Johnson. She never came to school though. Late in the year she walked into class and I didn't even recognize her. I asked her to sign to the guest book. Anyway, during her four years of high school, she missed a total of, get this, 500 days exactly! Ever since then, I started referring to her as "Daytoya 500." Coincidentally, she works at AutoZone now. CORNY!

123. One of my students once told me that I "got on her last nerve." So I asked her "Well then, who got on your second to last nerve?" She said that I did but I explained to her that it clearly couldn't have been me since I was so busy getting on her last nerve. In short, her last nerve was my alibi. She didn't mouth off to me anymore that day. Oh, but tomorrow is always a new day.

124. Some guy in my summer class had a cube block shaved in the back of his head. So I asked him "If you get a fever, then does that mean the block will be hot?" He said "I don't know, maybe." So then I just replied "Holla back, playa." And class resumed.

125. I was at a two-day education conference out of state one time. On the morning of the second day, I was having breakfast with a bunch of other teachers that I had just met. One guy said "I really loved our breakout sessions yesterday, I now have a great vision for my school." Now, I am so not a morning person so I just turn to this guy with my half open bloodshot eyes and said "I *see* your point." I guess it was one of those things where you just had to be there. Oh wait, I was there and it still wasn't funny. Oh, well, as long as it was almost funny, it is good enough for this book.

126. At that conference I learned how to put together math strings to have my students figure out what number comes next. For example, you start with a number, then you do something to it, and keep going eight or nine more steps. At the end, everyone in the class should have the same number. Well, I was right in the middle of putting together a real good math string at home when suddenly my cat jumped up and swiped it from me.

127. When Melanie, a friend of mine, was in school with me, she was always falling behind and asking for her make-up work. I just rang into her recently and found out that she now works for Mabelline.

Five
Movies and Shows

1. Why wouldn't it be a good idea to see the movie *U–571?*
   If you haven't seen the first 570.

2. *We Were Soldiers.* Cool. Good movie. Well, apparently now they're actors.

3. I just saw the movie *The Day After Tomorrow* the day before yesterday.

4. *The Day After Tomorrow* opened Friday, May 28, 2004. What was cool was Wednesday, May 26 because that was the only day that you could say *The Day After Tomorrow* opens the day after tomorrow. I remember saying that to pretty much everyone I came in contact with that day. It was interesting seeing people's reaction because some knew what I was talking about but others didn't. The ones that didn't have a clue thought I was nuts that day. Good thing they only thought I was nuts *that* day.

5. *Gone in 60 Seconds.* Great movie . . . yeah, all minute of it. The previews were longer than the movie.

6. *15 Minutes.* There's another one. Yeah, pretty quick movie. I just saw it a half hour ago. Watched it twice.

7. On the flip side, which movie is longer: *Batman Forever* or *Infinity*? I don't know, I've had them both on for years and neither one is over yet.

8. My wife says that we saw *Forgotten* together. I don't know. I can't remember a thing about it.

9. One night I saw *Remember the Titans* followed by *Forgotten.* Later that night I had a very strange dream but I can't recall what it was about. I also need to see *Remember the Titans* again since I forget how it ended. As it turns out, I guess I did see *Forgotten* after all.

10. Someone asked me if I saw *Don't Say a Word* (starring Michael Douglas) and I said that I did. Then she asked me what it was about and if it was good so I replied "I'm not gonna tell."

11. *House of Wax.* Now there's a quality film. I can't believe it didn't get four stars. I wrote the producer and suggested that they give out free candles on opening night. He never took my advice. In retrospect I don't think it would've helped much.

12. If they combined *O Brother, Where Art Thou* with *Dude, Where's My Car,* it would've been called: *O Brother Where Art Thou Car, Dude?*

13. I just saw *The Interpreter* and I didn't understand any of it. Maybe subtitles would've helped.

14. *Blair Witch Project* was just on national T.V. recently. Since they had to edit out the foul language, the entire movie was only like thirty-two minutes long.

15. When *Ocean's 11* first came out, I thought it was going to be a movie about Billy Ocean's greatest hits. Then I realized that it would've been called *Ocean's 3* if that was the case. Then the sequel came out and instead of *Ocean's 12* I thought it was going to be called *12 Continents*.

16. *2 Fast, 2 Furious:* Good movie, but is it just me, or do those dudes shift WAY too much when they race? I mean, C'mon, how many times do you need to get into 5th gear? There is this one scene where they're doing like 120 mph, but in an attempt to try and look cool, they all *keep* shifting. I thought this one guy's car was a seventeen speed. Ridiculous.

17. Someone told me that they saw *Proof* with Anthony Hopkins. I said, "Oh yeah, prove it." I wonder if you can get a discount to the sequel when it comes out if you show them your proof-of-purchase from the first movie. Looks like I'll be writing *that* producer now.

18. *Dodgeball* was pretty funny. I heard that they were working on the sequel. Do you know what it will be called?
Kickball.

19. Why did Alyssa Milano choose to act in the T.V. show *Charmed?*
Because she felt a little helpless while filming *Embrace of a Vampire.*

20. *Gladiator* was good. When Russell Crowe met the young Caesar (that killed his wife and son) at the Coliseum and Caesar asked him to reveal his identity . . . Crowe said "I am General Maximus Zurillus, Commander of the Northern Army, etc."
I disagree. I think he should've said "I am Gluteus Maximus Zurillus and I'm gonna kick your butt."

21. There is another scene from *Gladiator* where Maximus (Crowe) fights this famous dude who comes out of retirement. Anyway, this huge guy is being announced as having an "undefeated" record. I sat there and thought: Isn't *any* gladiator who is still alive going to be "undefeated?" As soon as you "lose" as a gladiator, the way I understand it, you're pretty much toast.

22. In the movie *Enemy of the State* there is as scene where they're trying to figure out who "Brill" is. The Congressman got the video from the convenience store, focused in on him and said "Freeze and process for face recognition." They're all looking at each other puzzled and I'm jumping up and down hollering at my T.V. "Oh for crying out loud . . . IT'S GENE HACKMAN. HELLO!"

23. I just saw *Ghost Ship* recently. Wow. That movie gives a whole new meaning to the term "blood vessel."

24. From the previews I could tell that *Eyes Wide Shut* was going to be a real eye-opener. I'm not positive though. I still haven't *seen* it yet.

25. They just started shooting the third *The Hills Have Eyes* movie. *The Hills Have Eyes 2* came out in 2007 but then the follow-up to that one will star Nicole Kidman. It will not be called *The Hills Have Eyes 3* though. They plan on calling it *The Hills Have Eyes Wide Shut.*

26. I watched *Field of Dreams* and that night while I was sleeping I dreamt that I was a farmer.

27. I'm still waiting for the sequel to *Footloose* that they said was coming a long time ago. I believe it was going to be called *Fancy Free.*

28. They did finally make a sequel to that Sharon Stone movie *Sliver*. It's called *Gold—better late than never.* Or maybe I'm just kidding. Who knows.

29. *Buffalo 66* was made in '98. I watched it in '04, even though I didn't see the first sixty-five. This low budget flop was so good, that it earned zero stars.

30. Has anyone seen Jessica Biel since she made *The Illusionist*? I'm starting to worry. Man, she played that role to perfection.

31. I went to the theatre to watch *Beerfest* and I was carded. They let me through but the dude behind me was only twenty and they didn't let him see it. Maybe next year, dogg. Now after having watched

it, the guy should consider himself lucky. He definitely could do something better with that seven dollars.

32. *Beerfest* is such a bad movie that you actually have to be pretty wasted just to tolerate it. So, by comparison, if you can put up with my corny jokes, then you will have no problem sitting through this movie.

33. In the movie *The Perfect Storm* with George Clooney, it would've taken nothing short of a mackerel for the fishing crew to survive that mammoth storm.

34. In the movies *Spiderman* and *Spiderman 2* there were absolutely no special effects done with a computer. Yeah, and FEMA did an awesome job in responding to Hurricane Katrina victims.

35. *The Quiet* and *Crank* were playing at the same time in a theatre. Some people in *The Quiet* theatre were upset that they were being shown right next to each other. During the loud scenes of *Crank* a mime (who was watching *The Quiet* right next door) kept banging on the wall whenever *Crank* got loud. I don't think anyone heard him through. After the movie, the mime complained to the manager of the theatre, but the manager acted as if he didn't hear him.

36. I saw *The Pursuit of Happyness* one day then later that night I watched *The Texas Chainsaw Massacre.* I was a very confused person after that and proceeded to send people mixed signals for the next couple of weeks.

37. In the movie *In Her Shoes* Cameron Diaz who plays "Maggie" was talking to her grandma about needing $3,000 to go to New York. She said, "I want to go to New York and become an actress, I think that I could be quite good at it." I was thinking "Well, hello . . . I believe you already are. You're one of the highest paid actresses in the world for crying out loud!"

38. I will bet you anything that you haven't seen *Two for the Money* as many times as I have. How much do you want to put on it?

39. I just don't know about that movie *Honey, I Blew Up the Kids.* personally, I don't support the blowing up of any children. I've heard of kids getting exploited and I thought *that* was bad enough; but now they're getting exploded? Absolutely ridiculous. Then they had the nerve to only give it a rating of "PG." A movie like that could cripple people psychologically for life.

40. *Turner and Hooch* is a pretty awesome movie . . . if you love watching a dog slobber about five gallons of his nasty saliva everywhere. I love dogs but I couldn't finish watching this one. The girl I was watching it with at the time worked at the Humane Society and it was even making her gag.

41. If they made my life into a movie, it would be called . . . Oh wait, they already did. It is *Benchwarmers*. I would have to say that I am much more like Clark than Gus Bus though.

42. In the movie *Flightplan* what did Jodie Foster do when she was being chased by the Air Marshal? She ran until she found the airplane's panic room.

43. I just saw the movie *Torque*. It reminded me of what everyone used to call me when I was in school. Good thing they only called me that back then (yeah, right).

44. In the movie *Oh, God! Book II* the school psychiatrist was interviewing Tracy (the little girl who was seeing and talking to God). When she found out that Tracy actually saw Him, she asked her "What does God look like?" Tracy said "Well, He wears glasses, has gray hair, and he's a very nice looking man." What Tracy should've said was "Well, I have to say that He sure looks an awful lot like George Burns."

45. Vince Vaughn and Jennifer Aniston starred in *The Break-Up* and shortly after it came out, they really did break up (in real life). OK, didn't they learn anything from Ben Affleck and J. Lo? At any rate, Vince has been desperately pleading to the film company to produce a sequel and call it *Getting Back Together*. They informed him that it wouldn't help his personal life and that it would actually produce the same results as if they starred in *Staying Broke Up*.

46. My ex-girlfriend and I went to see the movie *How To Lose a Guy in Ten Days* at the theatre. A couple of weeks later, she broke up with me. Fellas, don't see this movie with your significant other if you want to stay with her. Or, maybe it was just me, who knows.

47. In the movie *Anchorman* the best scene was when all of the networks met up for the big brawl in the parking lot. It would've been even better though if when Ben Stiller's Hispanic news team showed up, Vince Vaughn beamed him in the head with a dodge ball. I was surprised that didn't happen given their history.

48. There is a rumor that they are discussing a sequel to *8 Mile.* I think that it will be called *9 Kilometers.* There was originally some concern that this movie would be considerably longer than the original, but after further analysis, eight miles is still longer than nine kilometers when considering the conversion ratio. So, it's all good.

49. The movie *Signs* (starring Mel Gibson) was pretty good. I liked watching Ebert and Roeper go over all of the positives and negatives about it.

50. Rocky Balboa came out in December, 2006. Plans for *Rocky Balboa II* are already under way. So who is old Rocky battling now? Larry Holmes? Or is it maybe "Smokin" Joe Lewis?

51. What is the official drink of the new movie *The Number 23?*
Dr Pepper.

52. I had a vision in July 2006 that Sandra Bullock's next movie was going to be called *Premonition* and it was going to open in theatres on March 16, 2007.

53. My wife just rented the movie *Flicka* and we watched it together. She really liked it but I just

couldn't get into it. I think that it should've been called *Chick Flicka.*

54. What happens if you are listening to the soundtrack from the movie *Infinity* and it starts skipping? The result would be a repeating decibel.

55. There is a popular rapper called *Freeway.* I'm surprised that none of his hit songs were on the *Rush Hour* soundtrack.

56. Fictional story; On the show *Deal or no Deal* a contestant had to pick one more case, but he couldn't decide. He then asks Howie Mandel "So, what number do you think I should go with?" Howie replies "Hey man, whatever blows your hair back."

57. I've been writing a script for a new show. I call it *Seasons* and I'm getting ready to send it out to the major networks. It's pretty cool. In one calendar year, there are four seasons of it. There will be this huge build-up for the season finale, then the very next day, the new season begins. The storyline is built around the life of a meteorologist.

58. I wanted to watch the T.V. show *Lost* the other night and I was flipping through the channels, but I couldn't find it. I guess I sort of felt a little, well, you know.

59. There is a new show on HGTV called *Hidden Potential.* it was supposed to he on a 8:00 and I was on the right channel, but I still had trouble finding it. Weird.

60. There is a show out called *Numbers*. I wonder *how many* people tune in to watch it?

61. I'm not sure why they named that big hit show *Friends*. Monica and Chandler end up getting married. Then, Ross and Rachel pull a Brittany Spears and get married in a drunken state only to divorce, have a baby, and end up together in the end. Maybe the show should've been called *More than friends*.

62. I'm a huge fan of the reality T.V. show *The Biggest Loser*.

63. I have a lot of respect for professional river dancers. I tried to do that dance one time and it wasn't pretty. I managed to trip myself and fall flat on my face. That group "Celtic Spring" from the first season of *America's Got Talent* has a good chance of working for the *Riverdance* show someday (Michael Flatlay's group). I mean, let's face it, they've already got their foot in the door.

64. Speaking of *America's Got Talent* I just saw the finale and the vocalists of "At Last" were very good. However, whose bright idea was it to have those drummers pound away about halfway through their song? Their vocals *are* their talent and the only thing those booming drums did was totally drown them out. I am a drummer and I still objected to their overall performance. There is a place for drums but not six super loud kettles when the emphasis is supposed to be on the singers.

65. Oh, and it was great to see *Quick Change* finally do

something different. NOT. At the very beginning David made a bottle of cheap wine disappear. Whooptie flippin doo. That was the only thing different. I'm with Piers on this one. I wish "Quick Change" *would* change. I was blown away the first time I saw their act, but it's like a comedian that keeps trying to tell you the same joke over and over again. Other than that, they were great. The other magician who changes it up every time should've made the finale.

66. What was Peter Falk's character, Columbos's profession?
He was a private glass eye.

67. *The Young and The Restless* is one of the longest running soap operas that is still playing. I'm wondering how much longer they can keep that title. Pretty soon, they will have to change the name to *The Old and The Resting*.

68. Other soap operas that have been on T.V. forever are also going to need to change their names if they stay on the air. *General Hospital* should change their name to *General Nursing Home, All My Children* will need to become *All My Great Grandchildren,* and *One Life to Live* will have to be renamed to *One Afterlife to Live.*

69. The T.V. show *House* has taken a hit with the ratings lately. It is obviously not feeling, I mean doing very well. As a matter of fact, the show was actually diagnosed with "shingles" recently. Perhaps that is why it has been sluggish in the ratings.

70. *Baywatch* was the most popular T.V. show in the world for a while. C'mon, who are they trying to kid with the title? With all of the hot actors and actresses on that show, who is watching the Bay? I think the show maybe should've been called *Peoplewatch.*

71. Why did Farrah Fawcett leave the hit T.V. show *Charlie's Angels?*
Because she felt that the script was getting too watered down.

72. I'm pretty excited about the new show on Showtime called *Dexter.* It is actually going to portray the lives of my parents and grandparents. OK, maybe not.

73. They say that they can't do that *Joe Millionaire* show again since everyone has seen the deception of it. I have an idea . . . just change the name to *Joe Billionaire.* That should work, shouldn't it?

74. On the show *The Bachelor* when they have the rose ceremony, it is always amusing at the conclusion. When there is only one rose left, the host always steps in and says, "Ladies, this is the final rose this evening." I'm thinking "Really? No way. I'm so glad that guy told me because otherwise I would've had absolutely no idea."

75. It's a good thing that *The Bachelor* doesn't lead any of the girls on or anything. There's nothing like starting a lifelong journey with your future wife than cheating on her with twenty-four other drop dead gorgeous women on national T.V.

76. Don't ever let a bad day get you down. Just remember, it could always be worse.
You could be Taye Diggs during an episode of *Daybreak*.

77. Have you ever seen the annual Scripps National Spelling Bee on ESPN? These eleven-year-old kids are getting these ridiculous words that I can't even pronounce and nailing them. They're asking what their word's entomology is . . . I'm thirty-four years old, a teacher, and I don't even know what the *word* entomology means. Well, I do now of course but not when I first started watching it.

78. Which T.V. show did the country music band "Little Big Town" make an appearance on?
Medium.

79. I applied to get on the new NBC show *Identity* but I was just informed that my application was stolen.

80. I actually auditioned for the new hit T.V. show *Heroes* and my audition went so poorly that they informed me if the show was called *Zeroes* then I would've gotten the part.

81. My landlord took my wife and me to see the production of *Rent* at the Playhouse Theatre. They haven't put that show on there in over twenty years. I guess you could say that "Rent" was overdue.

Six
Unknown Mysteries

This chapter is rather unique in that up until now, I have provided an answer to all jokes that posed a question. Everything in this section is a little off the charts since not only do I not have an answer, but everyone that I have asked these questions to has not given me a straight answer or explanation either. The answers are truly "unknown." If anyone reads one of these who possesses the knowledge to help me out, please contact me. I would appreciate it. Do the aliens hold the answers? Will we all find them out in the afterlife? (These are two "warm-up" questions to help get you started.) I even posed some of these questions on www.ask.com and all they could say back to me was "Go away cornbread, leave us alone." OK, here we go. . . .

1. If a catch-22 is a lose-lose situation, then does that mean that a throw-21 is a win-win situation?

2. Why do people laugh whenever you're not trying to be funny, but then when you try, they don't laugh? Maybe that only happens to me.

3. If no two snowflakes are alike, then how about two cornflakes? Or even dandruff flakes . . . are these all unique?

4. Why are the first four letters of missile m-i-s-s? Shouldn't they be called "hittiles" instead?

5. If the freeboard on a boat is damaged, then does it cost anything to have it fixed?

6. Why do non-profit organizations send out coins in their request for donations?
I just had one the other day send me fifteen cents and they were asking for twelve dollars. I thought "Wouldn't it have made much more sense (no pun intended) if they just kept their money and solicited me for $11.85 instead?" I don't get it. Then another one sent me a pen and in the letter they were talking about how badly they needed back to school supplies. I was thinking "Well, don't send me the doggone pen, I've got like 800 of 'em in my kitchen drawer! Why on earth would you send something out that you desperately need to someone who can't stand the sight of it?"

7. Is it possible to get nightmares while daydreaming? If you do have bad daydreams, then why aren't they referred to as daymares?

8. If someone tells you to get a life, does that mean they want you to buy the cereal or the board game? I went and bought one of each so now when people tell me to "get a life," I say, "That's OK, I have both." I always catch a weird look when I say that.

9. They say that life begins at forty. Well, if that's the case, then at age thirty-four am I still considered to be a fetus?

10. A lot of people say that they live in the past. How can they do this without a working time machine?

11. Why are classified ads called classified? They are printed in billions of newspapers all over the world every day. That doesn't sound very "classified" to me.

12. If you're sending someone a "Farewell, have a safe trip" card, then why is it still called a greeting card?

13. Why do people spend huge amounts of time looking for just the right greeting card when the person we give it to doesn't really read it anyway? Does it really matter what the words say if you stuff enough cash inside it?

14. If a Roman candle is a dud, then is it still technically a firework? Maybe duds should be called "Fire-didn'twork."

15. When people watch fireworks, why do they act like it is the first time they've ever seen them?

16. If grass is the most abundant weed on the planet, then why do people get arrested if they are caught in possession of it? Kids can play on it, teenagers can mow it, but if it is in your pocket during a random frisk then you are in BIG trouble. That makes a lot of sense.

17. If you plant a light bulb, would it still need sunlight to grow, or would it be self-sufficient?

18. If the Internet is called the "Information superhighway," then why is it called "surfing the web?" Shouldn't it be called "driving the web" instead?

19. Why does Match.com and Eharmony.com try to match people up that have a lot in common with each other? Isn't it opposites that are supposed to attract?

20. Why do radio stations advertise on billboards? Is the best billboard in the world still going to be enough to change what kind of music people like?

21. Why are there so many comedy channels on my Sirius satellite radio?

22. Why do people call in to radio stations and request the current #1 song? Isn't it going to be played in the next twenty minutes anyway?

23. If green is one of the oldest colors, then why is it still called green?

24. Why are black lights purple? Does that mean that purple lights produce black rays?

25. Why aren't blueprints drawn up on construction paper?

26. Why are there water softeners? Why do they even exist? I thought all water was soft.

27. Are your dishes happier if you wash them with "Joy" dish soap?

28. Why is it that nobody ever buys any windows when they go window shopping?

29. Can you have more than one "Cingular" phone? If so, what would be the plural for Cingular?

30. Do Rotary Clubs have touchtone phones?

31. If a cell phone company charges you $39.95/month for 900 free anytime minutes, then why do they call them "free" minutes?

32. If they charge $150 to skydive, then why do they call it a free fall? Maybe it should be called an expensive fall?

33. Why are airfares so ridiculously expensive that it is completely unfair to the average consumer? Maybe they should be called airunfares?

34. Why do people say that the sun either rises or sets (goes down)? The way I understand it, the sun hasn't moved much in the last oh, I don't know, two billion years.

35. If Pluto is no longer a planet, then is plutonium still a radioactive metallic transuranic element?

36. If you have a sense of humor, then does that mean you have six senses?

37. Why are feet so cute on baby boys so ugly on grown men?

38. Why do they make shoes for infants? Also, why do people buy them? I've never seen a three-month-old walking around and in need of shoes.

39. Why does the funny bone hurt so much when you bang it on something? Maybe it should be called the excruciating bone.

40. Why are the funny bone and the humerus bone two different bones?

41. If a skeleton gets arrested, would it wind up in the joint?

42. If the human body is 90 percent water, then why do we sink so quickly to the bottom of a pool or lake? What is the other 10 percent bowling ball?

43. Why does Kaufmann's (now Macy's) keep having these "Biggest Sale of the Year" sales? Aren't you only supposed to have one of those per year?

44. What is up with stores that offer a "free gift" with the purchase of something? Is that supposed to differentiate them from their competition who offers "expensive gifts" with their merchandise?

45. Why is the "big sale" always at the store that's on the opposite end of town from your house? Does anyone ever live close to the store with all the good buys? It must be nice if you do.

46. Why doesn't the Salvation Army ever go into battle?

47. Why do grocery store cashiers still highlight twenties and fifties that have already been checked?

48. Why do the express lanes always move so slow? Come to think of it, maybe I'm asking the wrong question. Maybe I should be asking: Why do people check out in twelve items or less, cash only lanes when they have thirteen items or more and then pay by check? I think stores should start charging these people double. Just take their total and hit X2, maybe that will make them think twice about slowing everybody else down.

49. Students don't ever date tests. So I'm wondering, why do they cheat on them?

50. Why do students who miss like twenty days in a row all of a sudden decide to show up on test day?

51. Why is every teacher's name "Key?"

52. Why do second grade teachers teach the psycho game of hangman during "playtime?" It's a pretty morbid seed to be planting in young minds don't you think? Yeah, someone wins when they either guess the word or when we have successfully hung this poor innocent man and he is no longer breathing. Real nice. Incidentally, I understand that they will now be changing the name of this game to the "Saddam Hussein Game."

53. Why do educators call them the "Three R's" when clearly reading is the only one?
You would think that people in the education busi-

ness could have that one figured out by now. I have never called reading, writing, and arithmetic the "Three R's." I suggested to the NEA that they should change it to something like "The R.W. & A. Fundamentals" but what do I know.

54. Why do the sweetest girls in high school always fall for the bad boys?

55. If #2 pencils are the #1 seller, then why are they still called #2 pencils? I didn't think anybody (or anything) liked being second. Apparently they don't seem to mind I guess.

56. If you earn a bachelor's degree one year after you got married, then do you still have a bachelor's degree?

57. Why is the coast called a coastline? It obviously isn't straight and according to "Euclidean Geometry" all "lines" must be straight (via a ruler or straightedge). Perhaps a more appropriate name like "coastethasketch" could be a more appropriate name. Uh oh, my Microsoft word just red-flagged my suggestion. That can't be good.

58. How does Gotham City signal Batman in the daytime?

59. Why is the city of South Bend located at the very north end of Indiana? Did one of the founders get a little twisted around and lose his compass over there? Maybe it was one of Brittany Spears' ancestors thinking they were overseas or something.

60. If the power goes out in Manhattan, NY, then would the "Battery Park" still be lit?

61. Why is Rhode Island called Rhode Island? It is clearly not an island.

62. Why is New Jersey still called New Jersey? It has been a state since 1787. If something is like 220 years old, it doesn't sound very new to me. Maybe they should change the name of that state to: "Used to Be New 219 Years Ago Jersey."

63. There was an earthquake in California recently and it was San Adrea's fault.

64. If Chile is one of the hottest countries in the world, then why was it named Chile?

65. Why is gasoline called gasoline? It doesn't even closely resemble any gaseous matter.

66. Why do gas prices always go down the day after you fill up, only to go right back up again a week later when your tank is getting empty?

67. Why do gas stations slow the pump *way* down to a drip when you still have like forty cents to pump? It takes longer to pump the last forty cents than it does to do the first $29.60.

68. Why do gas stations have pumps that say "Prepay First?" Is that supposed to differentiate themselves from other pumps where you prepay last?

69. A local car dealership was advertising cars on sale at "dead cost." So what, as opposed to other lots that offer their cars at "live cost?" Also, why would they advertise dead cost when it is exponentially more morbid than what other dealerships offer? Great, let's get a new car at dead cost, and then the next day let's drive it right into a cemetery.

70. Why are highways that travel through valleys still called highways?

71. Why do people that are not speeding on the highway suddenly slam on their brakes when passing a police car? I don't get it. They are scared to death to get a ticket (even though they weren't even speeding), but they don't seem to care about the nine car pileup that they caused behind them.

72. Why are slow drivers oblivious to the fact that they belong anywhere BUT in the passing lane? Were they never taught which lane certain types of drivers are supposed to drive in, or are they just completely ignorant and/or defiant? What the U.S. Government needs to do is make it a Federal felony if you are going any slower than five mph over the posted limit in the far left lane. I need to get into politics when I retire. I will get people that need to change lanes to get the heck over. I might just get elected on that alone. Who knows. Crazier things have happened in this world.

73. Why do people who don't use their blinkers get mad at other drivers who don't use theirs either?

74. Why are hot peppers called chilies? Shouldn't they be called hotties?

75. Why is it called "Pepsi Free" when clearly they charge you every time? The stuff tastes so bad, it should be free. I don't even think they could give it away. I think I know what the free means . . . taste free.

76. Why do sandwiches taste better when they are sliced diagonally?

77. What if a load of goods such as fruit arrives half rotten? Should it still be called "goods?"

78. Why is it that when you have fast food and you're trying to eat in your car, you catch every light green, but every other time the lights are always red?

79. Does Popeye's Chicken cook their food in olive oil?

80. I went to Popeye's Chicken one time. Why don't they have spinach as one of their sides? I tried to order it but when they said that the don't have any I was shocked and disappointed to say the least.

81. If you can have your cake and eat it too, then can you have your coffee cake and drink it too? I'm not so sure. I tried once and started to choke on it there for a minute. I don't recommend drinking coffee cake.

82. Why don't brownies ever sell any brownies? They sell plenty of girl scout cookies but never any brownies.

83. How does Nabisco still manage to sell regular Oreos even after they came out with Double Stuf?

84. Why does the AA baseball team "Altoona" have their mascot named "Curve?"
Shouldn't it be the "Fish?"

85. In professional sports, why are "free agents" so expensive to get?

86. Do you think that sports coaches are insulted that flying "coach" on an airline takes a back set to first class? What if a coach flies first class? Could that get confusing for flight attendants?

87. Why do basketball coaches yell and scream at their players when they are up twenty+ points at halftime, but when they are losing, they are as calm as can be?

88. Why did Scott Skyles (former head coach of the Chicago Bulls) make it a team rule that his players are not allowed to wear headbands during games anymore? That has to be the dumbest team rule I have ever heard of in my life. What is so offensive about wearing headbands? You are just begging for your players to retaliate against that one. As a coach, you're supposed to pick your battles, not create them.

89. If Shaquille O'Neal is "Diesel" then is Dwayne Wade "Regular Unleaded?"

90. Why do boxers win "purses?" You would think that

they could come up with a more barbaric name for the prize money than that. It should at least be called something a little more masculine like man-purse or fanny pack. Yeah, that's much better.

91. In the NFL, why are the Indianapolis Colts in the AFC South division but the Miami Dolphins in the AFC East? I realize that Miami is east, but it is also a heck of a lot more south (than Indy).

92. Why are the Cleveland Browns the only NFL team without a logo or cheerleaders?
I won't even start on what else they are lacking.

93. Why is it that a very bad football team all of a sudden miraculously figures out how to play on the day you decide to bet against them?

94. When a football team is penalized for having an ineligible man downfield, my question is; "If he was so ineligible, then why was he even dressed and playing in the first place?"

95. When Penn State loses a football game at home, is their campus still "Happy Valley?"

96. Why does the "Big 10 Conference" have 12 teams?

97. Why did the ABC Family channel air *Cruel Intentions?* That movie has just about everything in it *except* family values. What kind of messed up world do we live in if we can't even let our children watch certain shows that are on a "family" channel? Then, a week later they played *Girl Next Door.* Yeah, there's

another one that's perfect to gather all the kids around and fire up the popcorn. Not.

98. Why did it take Hollywood seventeen years to come out with the sequel to *Roadhouse? Roadhouse* (starring Patrick Swayze) came out in 1989 but *Roadhouse 2* didn't emerge until 2006. I'm pretty sure it didn't take them seventeen years to make the first one. Seventeen days maybe.

99. Why are commercials always ten times louder than the program that you are watching? And why do they run the same ones fifty times in a row over and over again?

100. I just saw an episode of *House Hunters* on HGTV and I am still confused. How can someone kill something that is not even alive in the first place?

101. Why doesn't Curtis Stowe (the "Take-Home Chef") ever approach any guys in the supermarket? And why don't any of these women's husbands or boyfriends ever get mad that there are a bunch of strange guys in his house and totally flirting with his woman. I'm just waiting for Joey Greco and the "Cheaters" crew to pop in one of these times.

102. Why was William Shatner the host of the new ABC show *Show Me the Money*? Why didn't they get Cuba Gooding Jr. to host it? If they had, maybe it would've lasted more than three episodes.

103. Why does NBC air "Friday Night Lights" on Tuesday nights?

104. Why does NBC always show "SNL" reruns on Saturday nights? If they are going to do that, then shouldn't the change the name of the show to "SNNL?" (Saturday Night Not Live.)

105. Why do *Wheel of Fortune* contestants always shout their letters SO LOUDLY?
Do they seriously think that Pat Sajak won't hear them if they just say the letter they want in a normal voice?

106. Why do soap opera actors and actresses always kiss so loudly?

107. Why are soap operas called soap operas? I haven't heard any decent singing on any of them yet.

108. Why are soap operas so dirty? Maybe they should be called "Operas without singing and in need of soap."

109. The song that Reba McEntire sings at the beginning of her show is called "I'm a Survivor." So I'm thinking "if that is the case, then why didn't she get on that show *Survivor* instead of having her own show?"

110. Why do flies disappear off the face of the earth as soon as you grab a flyswatter? Then, why do they mysteriously reappear as soon as you set it down?

111. The early bird gets the worm, but the early worm gets devoured. So, it is really that beneficial to get the day started early? Personally, if I get a day off work, I get up at the crack of noon.

112. If a bird flies right through a government "No-Fly Zone," then would it be hunted down and dealt with?

113. How do electric eels survive in water? Isn't water a very high conductor of electricity? I'm surprised that they don't have a high suicide rate.

114. What would you compare a lobster to if it got too much sun?

115. If a tiger shark ate a catfish, then would it be considered a double cannibal? I know that fish already eat other fish, but this case is really pushing the cannibal envelope.

116. Do you think that on the ocean floor somewhere all of the fish hold their version of the Kentucky Derby with some of the top sea horses in the world?

117. Why don't squirrels get electrocuted when they run along live wires?

118. If a rabbit goes bald, then would it still be considered a hare?

119. Why do water buffalos live on land?

120. If a female laughing hyena laughs too hard, then will milk start squirting out of her nose?

121. If a lion killed one of its own in the group, then would the group still be called "a pride?" They may have to rethink their name whenever this happens.

122. If humans are like 500X's more intelligent than dogs (at least most humans are), then how do dogs just automatically know how to swim but us humans must go through extensive training to learn how?

123. How many cavemen died from cave-ins? The caveman who kept statistics on that actually died from a cave-in just days before he was going to report on it, according to his ancestors. Think happy thoughts people. Big daddy still loves you.

124. Why is an ultrasound called an ultrasound? Since its main objective is to see the fetus, then shouldn't it be called an ultravisual?

125. If Uncle Sam is the U.S. Government, then who is the aunt?

126. If it costs the U.S. Government 1.2 cents to make each penny, then why are they still making them?

127. Did the scientist "Ohm" ever practice meditation? You would think that he was the one who invented it.

128. If Donald Trump sells one of his parent companies to his son, then would it still be a parent company?

129. If Judge Reinhold is an actor, then does that mean there is a judge out there somewhere named "Actor?"

130. If Billy Joel commits a crime, then should he write a

new song and title it: "Not An Innocent Man Anymore?"

131. Why does Kid Rock rap? Better yet, why does he rap about being a cowboy? Can he just pick one and stick to it please?

132. Why are cowboys called cowboys? Aren't cows female? So, that's an oxymoron, right? Shouldn't they maybe be called bullboys instead?

133. How can country musicians keep coming out with new songs? Everyone has already written and performed pretty much every possible redneck hillbilly scenario known to man. I sure wouldn't want to be a new country singer these days trying to grow on soil that's already tapped out.

134. Why do musicians always say "1, 2" after they say "mic check?" What, by just saying "mic check" they still have no idea if the speakers are working yet or not?

135. Why do all girls hate their hair? Girls with naturally curly hair wish it was straight and girls with naturally straight hair curl it all the time. WHY?

136. Do women ever get infected with meningitis? If they do, do the doctors change the name?

137. Why are housekeepers called housekeepers? They don't own the place. Shouldn't they be called housedwellers?

138. Why are housewives called housewives? Clearly none of them are actually married to the house. At least I hope not anyway. I've heard of material girls but this is getting ridiculous.

139. Why do people continue to launder money when all it does is fade the colors and makes it much more delicate resulting in more tearing?

140. Why is it that the people you don't want to call you call all the time but the ones you want to call never do?

141. Are people with multiple personalities guilty of identity theft?

142. Why do some people who are complete failures as parents have their kids turn out to be successful millionaires but some parents who do everything right as parents have their kids turn out to be law breakers?

143. Why do unemployed people always work odd jobs? Why don't they ever work any even jobs?

144. Can an optimist still look on the bright side if their power goes out in the middle of a cloudy night?

145. Why are there so many people who are hydrophobics (having the fear of water)?
Didn't they spend the first nine months of their existence engulfed in it?

146. How would you be able to tell if a mime ever came down with laryngitis?

147. Why do people say "this week is flying by so fast" or "this week is dragging so slow"? Aren't all weeks exactly 168 hours long?

148. Why do first time poker players always get such beautiful cards?

149. Why do poker announcers call a pocket pair "wired" (which means unsuited)?
Aren't all pairs wired? If not, then there is something wrong with the deck.

150. If you get married and your spouse's brother is a policeman, would he be called your brother-in-law enforcement?

151. Why are illegal aliens called illegal aliens? They sure look human to me. By the way, if they are so illegal, then why don't they get arrested? Are aliens that jump from their planet of birth to other planets called "illegal humans?"

152. Why do doctors, who have an average of twenty-two years of education, have such poor handwriting?

153. Why are stockbrokers called stockbrokers? I mean, how am I supposed to have confidence investing my hard earned money with someone who has the root word "broke" in their title? Wouldn't they get a lot more business if they were called "stock-financialfreedoms" instead?

154. Why do rich people drive cheap cars and broke people soak all of their money into their sweet rides?

155. If knowledge is power, then do really smart people have to pay for electricity?

156. Why do some elderly women go out in public on a sunny day with their shower cap still on? Should we, the general public, inform them that it is OK to take it off now?

Seven
Miscellaneous

[Disclaimer: This chapter contains some of my funniest and some of my worst material ever. So I personally guarantee that you will almost laugh at some of these. Good luck.]

1. If you get into an argument with someone, why is it good to keep your cool?
Because it will come in handy on a hot summer day.

2. I was reading an article about B.O. in the local newspaper recently. I read the whole thing and I have to tell you, the article just stunk.

3. What does Welfare do if they have run out of funds?
They still provide lemonade.

4. I buried a time capsule fifteen years ago. The next day, I dug it up. As I was digging I said "Man, you know it just seems like yesterday when we were out here."

5. I was going to try some of my material on MTV's "Yo Momma" but my jokes are so corny that they might *charge* me the $1,000 for telling them.

6. I tried a paint by number once and when I was finished, my answer was 564. I guess as a "math" person, I misunderstood what they wanted me to do. As far as the picture goes, it looks pretty much the same as when I started it.

7. What should you do if you ever receive a scroll from a troll?
You should probably take a stroll down to your local nuthouse and check yourself in.

8. Why is it a bad idea to wear corduroy pants and a flannel shirt together?
Because you might burst into flames. That's extra bad these days since you really shouldn't be smoking either.

9. What did the drywall say to the 2 x 4?
"Hello there, stud."

10. I dressed up as a clown for Halloween one year. People just sort of looked at me funny.

11. I sleep power walk. I figure, since I sleepwalk, I might as well get a good workout in while I'm at it.

12. What is it called when a church purchases a building for the homeless?
It is a tax sheltered shelter.

13. Have you ever been so busy in your life that you don't even have enough time to make a "To Do" list?
Right now, number thirty-seven on my "To Do" list is to update my "To Do" list.

14. They say that the pen is mightier than the sword. I'm not sure if I agree with that. If I am about to do battle, unless the pen is loaded with some kind of C-4 or something. I think I'm going to go with the sword.

15. I'm thinking about starting a non-profit organization that is going to be dedicated to providing birthday and Christmas presents to underprivileged farm children. I'm considering calling it "Toys for Tater Tots."

16. I'm thinking about moving to an obscure out-in-the-country town, changing my last name legally to Voteforme, and running for Mayor. At an election speech, I wold just say "Hello, my name is Marty Voteforme and I would like everyone here to, well, you know." It would be a little weird talking to someone who didn't know me though. Some local guy would probably say to me "So you're the new fellow in town running for Mayor? What's your name?" I would simply reply "Voteforme." He would then come back with "Well, how the heck am I supposed to vote for you if I don't even know your name?" I would come back with "Dude, I just told you. It's Marty Voteforme. I was born to be Mayor in this here town."

17. I'm also thinking about picking up and moving to a different country, one that I have no idea how to speak the language, and becoming a cab driver.

18. My tip of the day: If anyone ever asks you if you can

keep a secret, then tell them "No." That way, they can't say back to you "Good, so can I."

19. My quote of the day: "Quotes of the day are often read but rarely change how we live our lives that day."

20. What is the main ingredient used in a cherry bomb? Citric acid.

21. I have never drunk a virgin daiquiri.

22. At our baby shower, my wife and I got 1.2 million receiving blankets. With the leftovers, we plan on knitting a quilt for King Kong.

23. Now that I'm a parent, I'm starting to get some peculiar things in the mail. Like the other day I got an offer for *Cookie* magazine addressed to me. On the outside of the envelope it said "The new magazine for the woman within the mother." Huh, I wonder what genius down at headquarters thought that Martin Drexler is a new mother?

24. Most yard sales have nothing but odds and ends. I want to be different so when I have one, I want to sell evens and beginnings.

25. I miss my garage. I have to brush the snow off my car in the winter now. I knew that I shouldn't have had that garage sale last year.

26. I was thinking about getting a tattoo of a razor on

my neck. That way, when I cut myself shaving, I can just tell people that my tattoo did it.

27. I got a tattoo of a back on my back. It's pretty cool. I tell people about it and even show it to them, but they don't believe me. So I guess I went through all that pain for nothing.

28. Why do they call them the "Seven Wonders of the World?"
Because everybody wonders what they are. I haven't found anyone who can name more than three of them.

29. In response to (the former planet) Pluto's recent downgrade, Walt Disney is expected to announce that Pluto is no longer a character at Walt Disney World.

30. My friends say that they waste a lot of time on the weekends. I told them that I would too but I don't know how to throw time away. I threw a watch away once but that didn't take but two seconds and now all I do is miss that watch. I don't feel that I wasted any time doing that though, just a perfectly good watch.

31. If watches were human, which kind would be most likely to wind up in a mental institution?
Seiko.

32. When does a stopwatch live up to its name?
When the little battery inside it dies.

33. Some politicians were discussing putting in a greenhouse at the White House. They want to grow violets, blueberries, green beans, and blackberries. They're only concern is that it might attract a bunch of yellow jackets. One Congressman has already spoken out against the plan. Turns out that he is colorblind.

34. What color tastes the best?
Orange.

35. What is the bravest color?
Fire Engine Red.

36. When people read my rap lyrics book, they laugh; but when they read my jokes, they don't laugh.

37. I just read the book titled *1994?* and it was about how the world will end in the year 1994. I tell you, that book is really flying off the shelves right now. Personally, I found it to be very informative. I'm not going to take a single day for granted anymore.

38. My wife and I were at a book store one time and I saw a book called *How to Win Any Argument* by Robert Mayer. Well, she said "it would be a waste of money." I replied "No it wouldn't." Needless to say, we started fighting over whether to buy this book or not. I said, "You see, this is exactly why I need this book. I'm tired of losing to you all the time!"

39. While we were there at the book store I did buy one by Brian Tracy titled *Eat That Frog* and subtitled *21 Great Ways to Stop Procrastinating and Get More*

Done in Less Time. I've had the book for about a year now and I just have never gotten around to reading it yet. I think I'll crack into it sometime next year.

40. Why is it not a good idea to buy a house from a painter?
Because it might be haunted by mineral spirits.

41. What do you call a ghost that rips off a jewelry store?
A polterheist.

42. What do you call a stagecoach that is haunted?
Stage fright.

43. What will happen if you don't make your house payments?
You will get arrested by the loan officer.

44. What happens if you get caught on camera stealing paper towels or dryer sheets and you're on the run?
You will get arrested by a bounty hunter.

45. There was talk on Capital Hill about legalizing marijuana recently. The national media immediately called for a joint news conference.

46. When I was in college I got pulled over for absolutely no reason whatsoever. At the time I had sort of a smart mouth so when the officer asked me for my license and registration, I showed him my fishing license and my Kent State registration form for fall semester. The cop got loud with me at this point so I informed him that he needs to be more specific when asking for certain documents.

47. Why are robots fearless?
    Because they have nerves of steel.

48. What do robots use when they go hunting?
    Machine guns.

49. Which card game is impossible for robots to play?
    Hearts.

50. What do robots use to make their bed?
    Sheet metal.

51. What do robots wear in the winter to stay warm?
    A steel wool coat.

52. There's a fine line between being funny and being weird. I said that to my wife once and then I said "Yeah, hunny, aren't you glad that I never cross that line?" She replied "Actually I wish you would cross the line *from* weird *to* funny sometime." I then said back "Ha! Good one hunny." I think she was serious though.

53. Come to think of it, I guess I do some weird things sometimes. Like, I take pictures of picture frames, then I frame them. Another time I bought some goldfish. Not the real fish . . . the crackers, and I opened them up and poured some in a bowl of water. I just wanted them to feel a little more at home. Then, just the other day, I bought some bookends and when I set them up, I placed a book *after* the second one. I'm such a rebel. I told my therapist about these things and he said, "Yeah, that's pretty weird." So I said "What's up dude, are you judging

me?" He said "Yeah, actually I guess I am." I need a new therapist.

54. I took twenty slips of paper one time and wrote "caution" on all of them. Later that night a storm was blowing through, so I took all twenty papers and tossed them in the air and started laughing. I think a couple of my neighbors saw me. I guess you could say that I was throwing caution to the wind. Now I finally know what that looks like.

55. During the summers when I'm not teaching, I work as a door greeter. Not at Wal-Mart or anything, in fact I don't even get paid. I just go around town to the local businesses and say "Hello" to the front doors. My therapist told me that I should stop doing that.

56. I have been soul searching my whole life. Fortunately, one lucky day while I was out shopping, I found a whole bunch of them at a "Payless" store. When I finally found my soul, I was overwhelmed with excitement. The saleswoman cautiously approached me, then looked at me funny asked "Excuse me, can I help you?" I exclaimed "No, that's OK, I'm SO HAPPY . . . I think I've finally found my sole!!"
She said, "Sir, if you don't calm down, then I'll have to call security."

57. About three years ago, my car was a Kia and my cell phone was a Nokia. So I had a Kia and a Nokia at the same time. I would say that they canceled each

other out but I can't figure out which one would be considered the positive one.

58. I'm wondering why Alltel has that blonde-haired guy doing commercials for their "My Circle" plan. It looks like he just rolled out of bed. With that hair-do he's got, you would think that it should be called the "My Crop Circle" plan. Hey dude, there's a new invention out now, maybe you've heard of it, it's called a comb.

59. Beware of cell phone salespeople. Some of them are phony.

60. Why do cell phones get great reception at prisons? Because prisons have a lot of bars.

61. Those new razor phones are a good example of today's cutting edge technology.
I just bought one recently since it came with a free can of shaving cream. The only bad thing is that I had to buy extra cartridges for it.

62. I keep getting text messages on my phone from some book. I don't know how it is typing and sending them to me but this annoying book keeps harassing me. I talked to my lawyer about it and he said that it should be an open and shut case.

63. When I was a kid I played the game "Life" with my brothers. One time I was a successful doctor and ended up winning the game. A week later we played "Operation" and I lost. My family was very disappointed in me. If I was such a great doctor just last

week, then why did I fail so miserably on "Operation?"

64. I went to get a board game off the top shelf of my closet one time but it was stuck in the bottom/middle of a huge stack of games. I had to be extra careful when pulling it down so that I didn't cause a small avalanche. When I quickly yanked it out, surprisingly all of the games stayed on the shelf except one. The Jenga game came crashing down.

65. What is the worst thing about a stalemate in chess? It puts a bad taste in both players' mouths for the rest of the day.

66. What kind of tool is used to cut puzzle pictures into pieces?
A jigsaw.

67. What did the puzzle piece say to the depressed puzzle piece?
"Hey, cheer up buddy. There is a place for you, you do fit in. Just not anywhere near me. Go, go over there."

68. One time I put together a puzzle of a person doing a puzzle. I was bored to pieces.

69. I went to a talent agent once and did my comedy act. He said "Well son, you really have to be more than just funny-looking." Then he referred me to a "lack of talent" agent.

70. I was talking to a friend of mine about becoming a

comedian and he said "Are you serious?" I replied "No, why, do I look like a satellite radio?" Then I added "Well, I hope I'm not too serious. Serious people aren't very funny."

71. When I was young, I was short and not very good at basketball. One year I led the league in shots blocked.

72. I'm a horrible golfer. Every time I hit the ball, it either slices or hooks badly. I tell you, that just really tees me off when it does that. Now, the good news is, I finally figured out how to hit the ball 250 yards. Unfortunately I guess that just means my ball is going deeper into the woods now.

73. I'm a horrible dancer too. At a high school dance, I tried to do the electric worm and somehow I managed to electrocute myself.

74. I went fishing one time and accidentally dropped my spare socks in the water. It wouldn't have been so bad if it didn't start raining. But of course, it did. Not a light drizzle either, we're talking torrential downpours. I got a little more nervous when on my way back to the car I bumped into another fisherman who called himself "Noah." Why was my walk back to the car five times farther than my walk out to the lake? Shouldn't it have been the same distance? Anyway, "Noah" says to me "Man, good thing my spare socks were nestled safe in my tackle box." I replied, "Yeah, that is brilliant. Mine were safe there too until my lure accidentally hooked and sent them

into the water in slow motion." All he could say was, "Man, socks to be you."

75. What do you call a fishing lure that professional fishermen use?
Probate.

76. What do boats do if they get damaged out on the water?
The next day they go see the dock.

77. What is it called when a U-boat makes a U-turn?
It is called a "W."

78. What happens if a boat with a full tank of gas stalls out on the water?
The local patrol gives it an undertow.

79. What part of a river is the loudest and most annoying?
The mouth.

80. What is the only bad thing about cruise vacations (besides getting food poisoning)?
Sometimes they can go a little overboard with their sales tactics.

81. Deep sea diving is very fun, just don't do too much of it. It has been shown that divers who dive too much often suffer from decompression which can then escalate into depression. OK, I think that joke just tanked.

82. What is the cleanest city in Ohio?
    Bath. My wife went to a baby shower there once. She
    said that there were a lot of car washes in town.

83. Detroit, Michigan is looking to attract families that
    have children with good motor skills.

84. Where in the U.S. is life insurance most expensive to
    buy?
    Death Valley, California.

85. Why is lower Manhattan named "Battery Park?"
    Because that is where the Energizer Bunny was fi-
    nally stopped. He was not able to "keep going" into
    the Atlantic Ocean.

86. What happens if you get injured while touring the
    Grand Canyon?
    The doctors will need to do an echocardiogram on
    you.

87. My uncle has a house in Key West, Florida. One
    night he locked himself out.

88. Someone set up several computer blogs out of Lin-
    coln, Nebraska. She is calling them "Lincoln Blogs."

89. A friend of mine recently told me that he and his
    wife just bought some china. I said "Wow, I didn't
    even know it was for sale. That must've cost a couple
    hundred billion dollars."

90. What is up with these in-flight films on airlines
    these days? Do they intentionally put the most bor-

ing thing they could find up there? If they're trying to put everyone out, they're sure finding some effective television to accomplish that. The last time I flew out to California, they showed a program on "the five best geology books ever written." It might as well have been on the five worst. Then they had the nerve to actually try and charge people $3 for headphones so that you can hear it! If they *offered* me $3 to take the headphones, I still would've turned them down. They even said "And for your viewing pleasure, we have an excellent program . . ." For my viewing displeasure maybe. I would've rather just watched commercials over and over again throughout the entire flight.

91. What kind of toilet paper do all major airlines use? White Cloud.

92. What should you wear if you ever go skydiving? Parachute pants. You may have to go to an 80s only store to find them though.

93. Crash test dummies are now being used to test new and innovative parachutes. Company executives said that the decision was a no-brainer.

94. There is one thing that I've always wanted to do . . . it's base jump. My friend asked me where I would do it. I said, "Oh, I don't know. The guy that sold me my life insurance policy works at a pretty tall building. After all, he did ask me to drop in sometime. Plus his name is Cliff, so it naturally makes sense to just do it there."

95. My friend and I were hanging out one day shooting the breeze. The BBs just went right through it. The next day, there was no wind, so we didn't shoot the breeze that day.

96. How can you tell if a cloud is in a lot of pain? If it starts passing hailstones.

97. If you ever think *your* mind is clouded, just think about the atmosphere's mind on a very overcast day. Yeah, could be worse.

98. I went to the bank last month and opened up a day-light savings account. It's a little weird how it works though. The account actually earns more interest in the summer, but less in the winter.

99. Where does the Olympic Committee store the medals before and during the games? They are stored in a large fire-proof safe known as the pole vault.

100. What should you do if you accidentally cut up the wrong credit card? Take it to a plastic surgeon.

101. All of my credit cards are TJ Maxxed out.

102. I have horrible credit. I still owe on my student loans after nine years. I went ahead and checked my credit score and discovered that I am losing.

103. My accountant suggested once that I should think

about opening up an IRA soon, but I told him that I'm a very good pitcher.

104. When I was in college, I was so poor that I couldn't even afford to pay attention to my professors.

105. I received a notice in the mail once that said "Congratulations! You just won $254,224 in our sweepstakes!" Yeah, except to claim my prize I had to send them a $12 processing fee. So I sent the reply back in but instead of $12 I included a note that said: "You know what, just go ahead an take the $12 fee out of my winnings. I can find a way to live with $254,212 instead." I haven't ever received anything back from them. Bunch of thieves.

106. I planted a rock garden in my backyard in hopes that it will grow some diamonds. I figure if I ever hit "rock bottom" in my life then maybe some nice fresh home-grown diamonds will maybe help cheer me up.

107. I also planted a bunch of acorn trees in my front yard for no particular reason one day. My neighbors thought I was nuts.

108. What do plants do during the World Series?
They root for their favorite team.

109. What should happen if a wild plant in the Panama Canal is dying?
It should undergo root canal therapy right away.

110. Tequila is distilled from a plant called the century plant. No wonder it has that aged kick to it. I'm

pretty impressed at the stamina of this plant. I am horrible at taking care of plants. I killed a cactus once. I even had a fake plant wither away under my care. I don't think that this plant would still be called the "century" plant if I were looking after it. Forget tequila, you would be lucky to squeeze Busch Light out of that bad boy.

111. Which flower will go down in history as being the most memorable flower?
The forget-me-not.

112. What kind of flower dominates in the wild?
Tiger lilies.

113. What did the branch say to the other branches that were picking on it?
"Leaf me alone."

114. I really don't know much about trees at all. If you point to one and ask me what kind it is, I will surely be stumped.

115. Remember that commercial that went "How do you spell relief? . . . R-o-l-a-i-d-s."
I'm afraid that I'm going to have to disagree with that. I believe it is spelled r-e-l-i-e-f. You would think that people with marketing degrees would know that.

116. What's up with these anti-depressant commercials lately? They are SO dreary. I think I know why they make them that way through. I guess they figure that even if you aren't depressed, you will be by the

time the commercial is over and as a result be in need of their product.

117. Have you ever fallen asleep listening to the radio, then by some weird osmosis thing, one of the commercials enters your dream? That annoying "Head On, apply directly to the forehead" one was playing while I was sleeping one time. Consequently, the awesome dream I was having was abruptly terminated and I started dreaming that I was hitting myself repeatedly in the head with a hammer. Yeah, that will make me want to go out and buy that product. What is that junk used for anyway? Is it some kind of moisturizer or something? Oh, that's right, they forgot to mention what their annoying product does since they're too busy screaming "HEAD ON, APPLY DIRECTLY TO THE FOREHEAD."

118. I just saw a commercial for Dell computers and the guy said "Just go to dell.com to order a new computer, it's that easy." Really? Well, I would but uhh, yeah, I don't have one. How am I supposed to get to dell.com without a computer? Because I have pressed every button on my microwave and that's not happening. Then I thought "Well heck, if I could get on dell.com then why would I? I obviously wouldn't need to order a computer." The commercial made absolutely no sense. The people that needed to do what they were asking couldn't do it and the people that could didn't need what they were selling.

119. I saw a commercial for a keychain that can record up to a twenty second message so that you can record reminders for yourself. They said "It's so simple to

use that even a child can do it." So I called the 800 number and asked them "So you're saying that it's so easy, even my child can record a message on it?" The operator said "Sure." Then I came back with "So what are you calling my kid, an idiot?"

120. I saw a billboard that said "Every 11 seconds someone switches back to the new AT & T that had left before." Yeah, that's believable. I can just see people waking up in the middle of the night screaming "I've got to call AT & T right now and switch back!" Those telecommunications people are just top on everyone's list to dial up late at night and first thing in the morning.

121. I e-mailed Calvin Klein my ad idea for Eternity. I suggested "Eternity . . . take a picture, it will last longer." I sent that like two years ago and just recently they finally replied, saying "Don't ever e-mail us again."

122. Even though I live in northeast Ohio, I have learned some Spanish simply by listening to commercials and calling certain businesses. For example, I know that "para Espanol, marque dos" means "for Spanish, press two." So now if I ever go to Cancun, that's like all I'll say the whole time. They'll be like "Hola senior, como estas?" I'll just reply proudly "Para Espanol, marque dos."

123. Why should you always have a straw with you when you're playing poker?
Because even good poker players need the occasional "suck out" on the river to win.

124. Satellite poker tournaments are pretty cool. Instead of getting a seat number to a table, you actually get your own lat and long coordinates.

125. I'm a pretty bad poker player. Usually, the only chips I have left in front of me by the end of the night are Ruffles.

126. One time (playing poker), I had the best hand and didn't even know it. Isn't that like bluffing in reverse? Anyway, this guy had two pair: King's and 6's. He was all confident thinking he had the best hand when I said "Well, all I have is a pair . . . and a third card that is eerily similar to my pair." Turns out I had three 8's. Oops, fumble. Except I'm such a moron, I still ended up losing the hand since apparently verbal declarations are binding or some crap like that. So technically, you have the hand you say you have. Whatever.

127. What does Hawaii have in common with a Las Vegas craps table?
They both have paradise.

128. Why are there more diapers sold in Las Vegas than anywhere else in the world?
Because there is an increasingly high occurrence of craps out there. (OK, hopefully that is the dirtiest joke of this book. I guess that one stinks whether you liked it or not.)

129. What do trash dumpsters in Las Vegas have a lot of?
Baccarats.

130. What is the nice thing about staying on the top floor of the Flamingo Hotel/Casino in Las Vegas?
You get a bird's-eye view of "The Strip."

131. One year when I went to Las Vegas I stayed at the Mirage Hotel/Casino. The only problem was, it took me three days to find it. I would see it, then it would be gone. One minute it's there, and the next it's invisible. I remembered thinking "Man, this Mirage is good. Frustrating, but good. Next time I think I'll just go to the Montecito. Maybe I'll bump into Molly Sims or Tom Selleck there."

132. When do people make moral mistakes?
When their conscience is unconscious. The general consensus is that there are consequences to having an unconscious conscience.

133. World peace is contingent upon the continents to continue to be content with each other.

134. If world peace is ever attained, who would sign the treaty?
The Continental Congress.

135. You know it is an extraordinarily bad day when you find out that your "ex" is expecting and you have to explain it to your girlfriend. She doesn't exactly want excuses, she just wants to explode your Ford Expedition expeditiously exactly at the Exxon station, then exit your life forever.

136. Some thief got caught stealing night stands from someone's bedroom last month while an old episode

of *Knight Rider* was on T.V. Last week he had to go on *Knight Court* as a result. Just last night his prison guard said "Lights out, good-night."

137. I ought to go to Ottawa and buy an ottoman for my pet otter this autumn. However, I would be considered to be an outcast from outer space and incur many out-of-pocket expenses. (OK, maybe I'm already considered an outcast from outer space but that's not the point.)

138. Poteen is a potent alcohol made from potatoes which means that it has more carbs than proteins and should not be consumed prematurely by any teens or preteens.

139. I have previously trespassed on private property in years passed. I possibly would've persisted, but one particular day I had a premonition that the police made me promise not to trespass on any property including private practice's premises (or else I would probably be put on probation). Presumably, the pressure prevailed and I promptly persuaded myself to stop my unproductive prowling.

140. Computers have RAM and ROM. People have REM (when they are asleep) and some have rum. Cars have rims. Therefore, someone who owns a computer and a car, and drinks on occasion (then passes out) will have RAM, REM, rims, ROM, and rum. Especially if he or she drives a Dodge Ram, then he or she would have ram twice. OK, that was pretty corny.

141. La-Z-Boy Furniture is now accepting applications from all freeloaders. So far they haven't received any.

142. At Bed, Bath, & Beyond they were advertising that maternity robes were on sale. I don't understand. Aren't all robes maternity friendly?

143. I like those divider thingies that you put on the conveyor belt after your groceries. In fact, I like to go to stores that sell them. I buy like four or five and put them on the belt last. One time the customer behind me grabbed one of the dividers that I was buying and I just started freaking out yelling, "HEY, HEY, HEY . . . THAT'S MINE!"

144. Two of the men's cologne products that Avon sells are "Driven" and "RPM."
Company executives are trying to see which one sells the fastest.

145. There have been reports of fights breaking out at stores over the "Tickle Me Elmo" doll as it flies off the shelves. It looks like the doll is having the opposite effect for which it was intended. Maybe it should be renamed "Instigate Me Elmo."

146. Blue Bonnett, Inc. showed a pretty impressive profit margarine last quarter.

147. Metamucil sales keep going up each year. Company executives are benefiting the most. Their constipation, benefits, and retirement packages have all greatly intensified.

148. Why was the homeowner mad at the ladder company that he owed a lot of money to? Because it had a lien on his house.

149. What do film companies and door manufacturing companies have in common? They both conduct screen tests.

150. There was a local computer store that was advertising "Top of the line notebooks for only $699." So I walked in there with the ad in my hand and a salesman approached me. He said "Hello sir, may I help you?" I replied "No, that's OK, I just wanted to point out that the 'notebooks' you are so proud to sell for almost $700, Wal-Mart is selling for like forty-five cents."

151. Just when you think that there is something that Wal-Mart doesn't carry, they continue to amaze you. They are selling fireplaces now. Only $699, fire not included.

152. The trucking company "Yellow" has their name written on orange-colored signs. What's up with that? I've thought about it and I'm going to start my own transportation company and call it "Orange." I will then have my company name printed on yellow colored signs. Then if the owner of "Yellow" asks me if I'm trying to mock him or something, I will just say, "I don't know buddy, what do you think? If you wouldn't have screwed up so bad in the first place then maybe I wouldn't have to cleanup your mess."

153. I like to buy my underwear at Goodwill. They sell

candy bars there too. Sure, they're half-eaten, but most of them are still pretty good. For a nickel apiece, you can't beat that!

154. Don't you just love how Columbia House offers 12 "free" CD's for only a penny? Then they say, oh by the way, it will cost you $6.99 shipping and handling per CD. Does it really cost them that much to send you something that weighs about 9 ounces? Anyway, if you're doing the math, that's 12 x 7 = $84 for those so called "free" CD's. Huh, that doesn't sound very free to me.

155. Which sport requires players to rack their brains constantly for the best strategy?
Billiards.

156. I told a bowling ball a funny joke one time and man, it was rolling.

157. Poker is officially a sport now. I find that somewhat amusing. It is probably the only sport in the world where you can be 150 pounds overweight and still be one of the best in the world.

158. Why are hockey games funny sometimes?
Because they are at times an example of slapstick comedy.

159. Which NHL hockey team is most likely to initiate a strike between the players union and the league if the players are unhappy?
The Tampa Bay Lightening.

160. Why is a golf course called a golf course?
Because it generally has a lot of rough.

161. I did the pole vault event for my high school track team. When my girlfriend broke up with me, she told me to just get over it.

162. I don't understand baseball betting lines. In the 2006 playoffs, the NY Mets were a . . . 110 underdog against the St. Louis Cardinals. So does that mean that Vegas thinks the Cardinals will beat the Mets by 111 runs or more? If so, I'm taking the Mets and the points all day baby.

163. After the NY Yankees got beat by the Detroit Tigers in the 2006 playoffs, Mike Fitzpatrick's article in the local newspaper puzzled me a little bit. He said "Maybe Steinbrenner (the Yankees owner), 76 and desperate to win another championship, finally will disagree (with replacing Torre as manager)." I thought *Desperate to win another championship? What on earth is he talking about? The Yankees have only won like 5,000 championships. If they are desperate to win a championship, then what are the Chicago Cubs feeling?*

164. I was listening to a football game on the radio one time and the announcers were commenting on how high up the press box was. One guy said "We're so high up that you can even see the airplanes." I thought "Really? How smart was that observation? I can see airplanes just fine too and I'm sitting in my lawn chair."

165. When Ohio State played Texas in the fall of 2006, it was a #1 vs. a #2 in the country match-up. In the pre-game, one of the announcers noted that Texas will be at a slight disadvantage having a young quarterback. That is when I called into the station and informed them that their quarterback, Vince Young, had been drafted back in June by the Tennessee Titans. So they did not in fact have Young at quarterback anymore. Gee whiz, you would think that guy would've known that if he is announcing the game.

166. The NCAA is coming down hard on the Gillette company because of allegations that they are involved in point shaving on major college football and basketball games.

167. Which NFL football team is in the most trouble financially?
The Buffalo Bills.

168. What is the official camera of the New Orleans Saints?
Canon.

169. In the NFC Championship game in January, 2007, why did the New Orleans Saints lose to the Chicago Bears?
Because Drew Brees never got his second wind. Come to think of it, shouldn't he be quarterbacking for the Bears anyway?

170. For being the MVP of the Super Bowl XLI, Peyton Manning was given a 2007 Cadillac XLR. In the

post-game presentation, he said, "Yippee . . . instead of having only fourteen vehicles, I now have fifteen!! A new Caddy is something that I needed so desperately. THANK YOU SO MUCH!!"

171. Where do aliens who are good with computers hang out after work?
At the space bar.

172. How did aliens get so smart?
By attending many universities.

173. What do aliens do first thing in the morning?
They take a meteor shower.

174. What do aliens use to hold up their pants?
An asteroid belt.

175. What do aliens get if they eat too much spicy food?
Asteroids.

176. What do aliens use to treat their asteroids?
Preparation X.

177. What is called when an alien goes a long time between bowel movements?
It must have a case of constellation.

178. What do you call an alien who is good at cutting hair?
It must have a background in cosmicology.

179. What kind of candy is most aliens' favorite?
It is a tie between Starburst fruit chews and the Mars candy bar.

180. What do aliens do when they want to prank other aliens?
They moon each other.

181. I'm going to keep roasting aliens until they come down and pay me a visit. They ain't gonna do nothin' though. (I am clearly not an English teacher.) If one of them does come down to confront me then I'll just say "You, are you George Foreman? I asked if you were George Foreman . . . I didn't think so, then get out of my grill."

182. What did Dracula say right after he won the lottery?
"Fangtastic!" (My wife, Melissa actually came up with that one.)

183. Even though I have never been abducted by aliens (yet), I was abducted by illegal aliens once before. They smuggled me to Mexico City and I was put to work there for $1,000 pesos an hour. That sounds like a lot of money, but it actually translates to only about thirty-six cents/hour.

184. There must be time machines in the future because my future "self" just paid me a visit and said that I better shape up or else I will get "lit up like a Christmas tree . . ." whatever that means.

185. What was the most popular kind of music back in the Stone Age?
Rock music.

186. Which band was the very first one to transfer their music from vinyl albums over to compact discs?
Genesis.

187. According to the Beatles, we all live in a yellow submarine. I'm not so sure if I agree with that. I used to live in a yellow submarine, but I don't anymore. I also know for a fact that a couple of my brothers have never lived in one. So to make the claim that everybody lives in one is just a tiny bit of a stretch. Maybe a lot of us do, but I really don't think that we all do.

188. Run DMC's song "Peter Piper" is arguably the best rap song of all time. Not.
They had another song called "King of Rock." What's up with that? That's like Metallica coming out with a song called "King of Rap."

189. When I was in high school my parents took away some of the music tapes that they thought I were potentially damaging for me to listen to. After that I proceeded to fight for my right to listen to the Beastie Boys.

190. There is a Nirvana concert next weekend. They want you to just come as you are.

191. I hate everything about the punk band "Three Days Grace."

192. In the song "Over and Over" by Nelly and Tim McGraw, history was made when hip hop combined with country for the first time. That's kind of like a heavy metal band and a gospel choir getting together to make a song. Nelly was the main guy in that song though. What did McGraw have, like three lyrics the whole song? He just kept repeating them over and over again. Drove me nuts.

193. Outkast made a #1 hit song called "Hey Ya" a few years back. Anyway, there is this huge build up in the middle of the song where the lead vocalist goes "What's cooler than being cool?" And right when you're expecting something awesome to happen next, the backing vocals hit you with "ice cold." Wow, that was brilliant. So that is the best they could come up with? And the song still went to #1? That makes a lot of sense. Just that part alone made the song a huge disappointment with me.

194. I just went to the music store and bought a Nickelback CD. With tax it came to $14.95, so I paid with fifteen dollars cash and got a nickel back. Well, actually, I guess that means I got two nickel backs then. Now if that's the case, then does that mean I should've just gotten a dime back? I'm confused now.

195. Why did Nickelback win Best Pop/Rock Album at the 2006 AMA's?
Because they had all the right reasons.

196. I was walking one time and I found a Red Hot Chili Peppers CD under a bridge.

197. The popular female vocalist Jo-Jo has a hit song where she tells the world that it is "Too Little, Too Late" for things to work out with her and her ex-boyfriend. Really? Isn't she like fifteen years old? About the only thing that is too late for her is to register for elementary school.

198. There are some country songs that I just don't get at all. There is this one song by Clay Walker that really drives me nuts called "If I Could Make a Living Out of Loving You" where he keeps repeating the same lyrics over and over. Walker continues with . . . "I'd be a millionaire in a week or two . . ." I was thinking "Well, if you love her that much then why would it take you two weeks to make a million?" If I could make a living out of disliking that song, then I would be a billionaire in a minute or two.

199. I had a broken record player when I was a kid. I used to play Duran Duran, ABBA, and Lisa Lisa and the Cult Jam records on it. Listening to them was almost as annoying as that joke was.

200. What are the most common stereotypes that people possess?
Aiwa, Bose, and RCA.

201. I just bought a huge entertainment center for my living room. It said "light assembly required." Yeah, right. There's the understatement of the friggin' millennium. That's like saying there is a light breeze when an F-5 tornado is tearing through the yard.

This project was *so* mammoth that there were directions for how to properly use the directions.

202. What happens if you put a humidifier and a dehumidifier in the same room and leave them both on for twenty-four hours?
Nothing.

203. I do not have a coffee table. I have a tea table instead, but it just broke recently. Why?
Because a tea table is not as strong as a coffee table.

204. The producers of the "ove glove" claim that it can withstand temperatures up to 540° degrees Fahrenheit. The commercial even says that you can turn logs in your fireplace. OK, well the glove may prevent the heat from hitting your skin, but when that glove eventually catches fire then you might have a slight problem on your hands.

205. I bought a Mr. Clean magic eraser about a month ago and put it in the bathroom closet. I went to use it the other day and I couldn't find it. It was not anywhere in the closet and I specifically put it there so that I wouldn't lose it. Now I know why they call it the magic eraser. Don't buy those things; they're a waste of money.

206. I bought a magic carpet one time from a Gypsy. Hours later it flew away. Don't ever buy one of those things, they're a waste of money too.

207. What is a good cure for shag carpet?
A lawn mower.

141

208. Why don't doors and windows ever get along?
Because doors always be frontin'. Also, doors think that windows can be a real pane sometimes.

209. What is the most talented item in the kitchen?
The skillet.

210. I would tell you what kind of deodorant my wife uses, but it's a secret.

211. What is the only "consumable" product that can last a lifetime?
Shaving cream. I'm still using the same can that was originally my grandpa's. I don't know how companies that make it stay in business.

212. I buy my Aim toothpaste at Target.

213. I buy my Tylenol Cold and Flu at Kaufmann's.

214. I really like that Comet cleanser. It works really well. I figure, hey, if it's good enough to clean the universe, then it's good enough for my toilet.

215. What happens if you ride the "Mind Eraser" at Geauga Lake too many times? You will get amnesia. I think that happened to me once, but I can't recall the incident at this time.

216. Why shouldn't you build log cabins near the equator?
Because they stand a good chance of getting cabin fever.

217. What are you guaranteed to come down with if you chew too much snuff?
Diphtheria.

218. What is the cure for chronic hangnails on your fingers?
Manicure.

219. I got mono once.

220. One year I had insomnia and narcolepsy at the same time. When I did finally get to sleep, I would dream that I was awake.

221. What should you do if you have a lot of problems?
Go to your local pharmacy and buy a bunch of solution.

222. That new drug for people with insomnia, Ambien, must be really good. The T.V. commercial for it even makes me tired. They have to be careful though not to make the commercial too tiring or nobody will buy their product. People suffering from insomnia would just record the commercial and keep replaying it. That would definitely be a lot cheaper that way.

223. What kind of drug is Ritalin?
It is a relaxative.

224. What should you do if you have a knot on your forehead?
Untie it.

225. My eyes are starting to go bad. In fact, they're so

bad, I'm illegally blind. I just hope I don't get arrested. I should see my friend who is an optometrist soon. I asked her once what led her to be a doctor. She told me that at an early age she had a vision to be an eye doctor.

226. What should you do if you have ringing in your ears? Answer it.

227. I have an ear drum set. It sounds really good.

228. My brothers and I were just hanging out one day. For no particular reason, one of them was mumbling words randomly. He just kept saying the word "things" over and over. My other brother looked at me and asked "Hey Marty, do you hear what Mike is saying?" I replied. "No." He asked again "he keeps repeating these same words . . . why is he doing that?" I just looked back at him and said, "I don't know, dude. I didn't even think he was saying anything. Maybe you're just hearing things."

229. It used to be that you were hip if you had a gold tooth. Now, you're cool if you have a blue tooth. I don't have either, so I guess I'm not cool. Oh, and if you have both, then does that mean you automatically have a green tooth?

230. All my life people kept telling me to follow my heart when making important decisions. Well, I tried that and all it ever did was keep leading me to my esophagus and other vital organs. So now, I'm not quite sure what to make of that advice.

231. I was originally going to put some appendices in the back of this book, but it turns out that I only have one and my doctor said that there was no need to remove it at this time.

232. When I went to renew my driver's license, they asked me if I wanted to be an organ donor. I informed them that I do not own an organ but I could donate my piano if someone was need of one.

233. The sun has been so hot these past couple summers that astrologers have actually discovered that it is s suffering from heat exhaustion.

234. I burned a CD the other day, but now it won't play. It got burnt too badly. I'm upset now because it had some hot tracks on it. Really hot.

235. Why did the business owner take his computer in to a chiropractor's office?
Because it slipped a disk.

236. Why did the computer have to go see an orthodontist?
Because it had an overbyte.

237. I send people subliminal e-mail and text messages. They suspect that they have messages in their inbox, but when they go to check, they're not there.

238. Why is it a bad idea to buy a used computer from the Nabisco company?
Because there will probably be a lot of cookies left on the hard drive.

239. My apartment burnt down one time and my computer was destroyed. I still can't believe it. I had firewall protection and everything. Ridiculous man. Don't ever pay extra for that crap. It doesn't work.

240. I just brought a computer and I paid extra for the Spy ware/Anti-virus protection.
I also paid extra for the three year warranty. On my way home I thought "Why did I get both?"

241. I tried to play that spider solitaire game on my computer but it wouldn't let me.
Apparently my mouse had eaten it.

242. What happens if you get caught hacking into government agencies with your computer?
When you get sentenced, you will get thrown into the "free cell" and put in "solitaire" confinement.

243. I am not very Internet savvy. I thought that www.Match.com was a website that you can go to if you wanted to burn a CD. I also thought that *www.EHarmony.com* was a place where aspiring musicians could go to form a band together.

244. Before I got married there were a lot of people chatting online and getting dates that way. They would always encourage me to try but you know, I just don't believe in computer dating. I never even saw a computer that I was very attracted to.

245. Why is computer dating so dangerous these days?
Because of all the potentially harmful viruses that

are out there, both human and nonhuman in origin. That's why.

246. I don't have a MySpace page, but if I did, under interests I would put: Geometry, Trigonometry, and Organic Chemistry. Am I cool or what?

247. I applied to work for the "Geek Squad" recently. They turned me down. The manager said that I had the geek part down fine, I just needed to learn a little more about computers.

248. I google searched the word "google" one time. I just sat there and watched my computer have a nervous breakdown. After about seven seconds, I think my search engine blew a head gasket because this bluish/purplish smoke started bellowing out of my CPU. Reminded me of the day my 1979 Malibu Classic died.

249. I was surfing the web and I caught my first tube on *www.youtube.com*, that is until suddenly my computer crashed.

250. Youtube.com is a pretty cool website that displays unknown talent in singing and dancing to help get them known, among other things. I actually logged on the other day and purchased some really nice socks from there.

251. I logged onto *www.computertraining.com* to take their online entrance exam. The first question they asked was: "Do you have a cable modem or dial-up?" Immediately after I answered "Dial-up" an instant

message popped up that said "OK, that will be all. Thank you for taking our online entrance exam. You *are* the weakest link. Goodbye."

252. When I was a kid I turned my bike into a car. I made it into a stick shift. It was pretty lame though, I would get all the way up to 8th speed but I would only be doing like 11 mph.

253. I rolled my lawn mower in to the local lube job shop one time. I asked if they could change my oil and they started laughing at me. Bunch of jerks.

254. What should you do if you are running low on self-esteem?
You should go out and buy a new Suzuki Esteem. That will give you a little more esteem. Don't just take one for a test drive either, that will just give you false hope. If you want the esteem, you must buy it.

255. What should you buy if you're not sure whether to buy a car or a truck?
An El-Camino. Just make sure you pay extra for the extended warranty. Piece of . . . well, you know.

256. I test drove a new Saturn and I have to tell you, those cars are really out of this world. I didn't buy one though. The sales lady was wearing seven rings. Not all on the same finger though.

257. I've been pricing some Hummers lately and the other day I broke down and decided what the heck, just get it. I have to tell you, I'm real proud of my new toy. I've been wanting a new Hummer ever

since LeBron was cruising his all around Akron. I run mine up and down the sidewalks in my neighborhood, do some sweet jumps with it. Napoleon Dynamite would be proud of me. I'm a little down today though . . . the remote just broke on it. Bummer.

258. I don't do U-turns. I do W-turns. I usually end up in somebody's front yard, but they're fun.

259. If gas goes back down to $2/gallon, I'm going to buy a whole bunch of it. I've got ten five-gallon containers. The only problem is, where will I store it? I could keep some of the full jugs in my trunk. Yeah, that's a great idea. No problemo, that is until someone rear-ends me. Whoops. That could get a little messy, and hot. I better not stock up on it then. If I do, with my luck the prices would just keep dropping and I would end up losing money out of the deal anyway.

260. I think I'm going to buy an SUV that can go off road. I really want that capability. That way I can drive it off the paved road and right into a swamp. What a great feature to have.

261. Chevrolet claims in one of their commercials that nine out of ten of their cars gets thirty miles per gallon of gas or better on the highway. OK, my question: "Are they still making Blazers and Suburbans?" Because if they are then maybe they should say eight out of ten instead. The only way either one of those tanks is getting thirty mpg is if they are coasting down a steep mountain or something.

262. What is the most popular car outside the city?
The Chevy Suburban.

263. On the first day of spring I plan on buying a Chevrolet Equinox.

264. I just saw a fairly late model Volkswagon Bug that had personalized plates saying "BC Bug." I thought to myself, "Man, the car doesn't look *that* old."

265. I was driving behind someone with a Mitsubishi one time that had a personalized plate saying: "UNVMYCR." I thought to myself "No, actually I envy the bank that holds the title to your car." What a cocky idiot.

266. My buddy just got a new Mercedes and he's all proud telling me about all the extras like heated seats and everything. Not to be outdone, I came back with "Yeah, well, my Kia has a heated . . . engine, especially in the summer when the temperature light pops on." Before the Mercedes he used to drive a VW but he really didn't like driving stick. I said, "Yeah, I'm great at driving cars with standard transmission . . . once they're in fifth gear."

267. At a used car lot I saw a car that had this written in the windshield of one of the cars: "98 Cruise Control." That's all it said. I thought "Well, heck. If I buy it, I only need one cruise control."

268. What happens if a car dealer sells a stolen car?
There will be a warranty out for his arrest.

269. One of my ex-girlfriends worked in cars sales. When I took her over to meet my parents they grilled her.

270. I invented a cutting edge new car alarm. It is vision sensitive. If anyone even so much as stares at our car for more than ten seconds, the alarm is activated. Next one I will work on will be a brain sensitive alarm. When it comes out, if anyone even thinks about stealing your car, the alarm will be activated. That one has about as much probability of selling as it does of even making it out into the market. Oh well, at least I tried.

271. Why is the road to success very frustrating at times? Because if you're in Ohio (especially northeast Ohio), then it is always under construction.

272. I took a cruise down memory lane one time, but I can't remember why I was there.

273. I used to work late night trafffic at a local radio station and one time a bad accident had the southbound lane on a highway closed. I was so tired though at 3:30 A.M. here is what I announced: "A five car pileup has 77S closed, so stay to your right." A few minutes later an angry listener called in and yelled "What's the matter for you? If it is closed then why are you telling people to stay to the right?" I replied "Well, first of all, it's what's the matter with you not for you, and secondly I guess I meant to say stay *way* to the right. Because I believe if you go off road for about a tenth of a mile or so, then you should be OK after that."

274. After that I became a DJ for a Jazz and Blues radio station. That is until one day I found myself in a deep depression. I woke up and just decided that I didn't feel like going in to work (kind of like Peter on *Office Space*). I don't even remember calling off. I had the blues so bad that I wasn't even feeling the phone enough to call in sick. I don't work there anymore.

275. When I was a telemarketer, this woman I was on the phone with was so mad at me. She yelled "I hate you guys, I want you to take me *off* your Do Not Call list." I replied "Well ma'am, I believe you're already off that list. In fact, that's probably a pretty good reason why we called you today. If you'd like, I can see to it that you remain off our Do Not Call list."

276. When I was in-between jobs, I decided to apply at the Russian Embassy as a guard. However, I pulled several muscles trying to do one of those ridiculous leg kicks. So, that didn't work out. Turns out, you have to be a former gymnast to be one of their guards.

277. I just let someone proofread my joke book. Forty-seven minutes into it, he let out a small chuckle. An hour and a half of total silence later, he handed it back to me and said "OK, I'm finished."

278. When I retire, I think I'm going to move down south and become a palm reader. I've thought about that often. I've always been fascinated with palm trees.

Conclusion

Well, I guess that just about wraps it up. I hope you enjoy some of my corny jokes, puns, and riddles. I was originally going to officially "wrap" this book up with a corn rap since I've been writing those too, but I guess you'll just have to wait for my CD to come out. I haven't even started recording that yet, so it will be a while. I just haven't had the time. Oh, that's right, I forgot . . . I should just follow my own advice and run to the store to buy more thyme. I highly recommend doing that since most people I know never have enough of it. Corny raps are available upon request if I ever see you in person. I'm no B. Rabbit or anything, but I'll do my best, even if it is a capella. I've been working on some beats too, but they're not ready yet. They've been growing in my backyard garden three rows deep and they're due to sprout in three to six weeks. I am prepared to drop a flow or two upon request. OK, on that note (no pun intended) this officially concludes my *Almost Joke Book*. Thank you for taking the time to share in my humor and I hope that I helped brighten up your day a little.

Peace and God Bless.

Sources

(Just one, so maybe I should've just said: "Source.")

The Illustrated Oxford Dictionary, Oxford University Press, Inc. 1998. (Various definitions quoted, used for entertainment purposes only, or lack thereof.)